MOST BELOVED BIBLE PASSAGES

For God so loved the world,
that he gave his only begotten Son,
that whosoever believeth in him
should not perish,
but have everlasting life.

JOHN 3:16

IDEALS PUBLICATIONS INCORPORATED
NASHVILLE, TENNESSEE

Editorial Consultant, James F. Couch, Jr.

James F. Couch, Jr., is an author and publisher with eighteen years of experience in the Bible publishing industry. After receiving a B.A. from the Univer-
sity of South Florida, he received an M.A. in Bible Studies from Dallas
Theological Seminary and Graduate School of Theology and has completed
postgraduate studies in Gifted Education. In addition to editing six different
study Bibles, Couch has authored *The Voice*, published by Royal Tapestry, and
Children's Bible in Story, published by Ideals Children's Books.

ISBN 0-8249-4077-6

Cover Photograph:
The Jordan River by Russ Busby, Photographer

Editor, Nancy J. Skarmeas; Copy Editor, Michelle Prater Burke;
Electronic Prepress, Amilyn K. Lanning

Copyright ©1996 by Ideals Publications Incorporated
535 Metroplex Drive, Suite 250
Nashville, Tennessee
Printed and bound in the U.S.A.

Designed by Gore Studio, Inc.
Film Separations by Precision Color, New Berlin, Wisconsin
Printed by RR Donnelley & Sons Company, Willard, Ohio

CONTENTS

In Biblical times, the Tigris River ran through the land known as Mesopotamia where the great ancient empires of Assyria and Babylonia once stood. Today, the Tigris flows through the lands of Turkey, Syria, and Iraq, pictured above. (Photograph by K. Scholz/Superstock)

LIFE

And
the LORD God
formed man
of the dust
of the ground,
and breathed
into his nostrils the
breath of life;
and man became
a living soul.

GENESIS 2:7

In the beginning God created the heaven and the earth. And the earth was without form, and void; and darkness was upon the face of the deep. And the Spirit of God moved upon the face of the waters. And God said, Let there be light: and there was light. And God saw the light, that it was good: and God divided the light from the darkness. And God called the light Day, and the darkness he called Night. And the evening and the morning were the first day.

GENESIS 1:1-5

Thus the heavens and the earth were finished, and all the host of them. And on the seventh day God ended his work which he had made; and he rested on the seventh day from all his work which he had made. And God blessed the seventh day, and sanctified it: because that in it he had rested from all his work which God created and made.

GENESIS 2:1-3

And God said, Let us make man in our image, after our likeness: and let them have dominion over the fish of the sea, and over the fowl of the air, and over the cattle, and over all the earth, and over every creeping thing that creepeth upon the earth. So God created man in his own image, in the image of God created he him; male and female created he them. And God blessed them, and God said unto them, Be fruitful, and multiply, and replenish the earth, and subdue it: and have dominion over the fish of the sea, and over the fowl of the air, and over every living thing that moveth upon the earth.

GENESIS 1:26-28

And the Lord God caused a deep sleep to fall upon Adam, and he slept: and he took one of his ribs, and closed up the flesh instead thereof; And the rib, which the Lord God had taken from man, made he a woman, and brought her unto the man. And Adam said, This is now bone of my bones, and flesh of my flesh: she shall be called Woman, because she was taken out of Man. Therefore shall a man leave his father and his mother, and shall cleave unto his wife: and they shall be one flesh. And they were both naked, the man and his wife, and were not ashamed.

GENESIS 2:21-25

And it came to pass at the end of forty days, that Noah opened the window of the ark which he had made: And he sent forth a raven, which went forth to and fro, until the waters were dried up from off the earth. Also he sent forth a dove from him, to see if the waters were abated from off the face of the ground; But the dove found no rest for the sole of her foot, and she returned unto him into the ark. . . . And he stayed yet other seven days; and again he sent forth the dove out of the ark; And the dove came in to him in the evening; and, lo, in her mouth was an olive leaf pluckt off: so Noah knew that the waters were abated from off the earth. And he stayed yet other seven days; and sent forth the dove; which returned not again unto him any more.

GENESIS 8:6-9A, 10-12

In one of the great acts of faith in Biblical history, Noah heeded God's warnings and built the ark that would preserve human life on earth during the great flood. Noah and his family shared the ark with two of each kind of animal so that the animal kingdom would also survive to repopulate the land once the waters had dried away. The Syrian shepherd pictured above continues the long tradition of animal husbandry that is recorded throughout the Bible. (Photograph by K. Scholz/Superstock)

A nd the LORD God planted a garden eastward in Eden; and there he put the man whom he had formed. And out of the ground made the LORD God to grow every tree that is pleasant to the sight, and good for food; the tree of life also in the midst of the garden, and the tree of knowledge of good and evil. And a river went out of Eden to water the garden; and from thence it was parted, and became into four heads.

GENESIS 2:8-10

The village pictured at right is located near Aleppo in modern-day Syria. Jesus' ministry had a profound influence on the people of the ancient cities of Syria. The Apostle Matthew said of Christ, "And his fame went throughout all Syria" (Matthew 4:24A). Christ's message continued spreading through the nation even after His death—it was on the road to Damascus, Syria, that the Apostle Paul was converted; and he later preached in another of Syria's great cities, Antioch. (Photograph by Superstock)

And the LORD said in his heart, I will not again curse the ground any more for man's sake; for the imagination of man's heart is evil from his youth; neither will I again smite any more every thing living, as I have done. While the earth remaineth, seedtime and harvest, and cold and heat, and summer and winter, and day and night shall not cease.

GENESIS 8:21B, 22

And God said, This is the token of the covenant which I make between me and you and every living creature that is with you, for perpetual generations: I do set my bow in the cloud, and it shall be for a token of a covenant between me and the earth. And it shall come to pass, when I bring a cloud over the earth, that the bow shall be seen in the cloud: And I will remember my covenant, which is between me and you and every living creature of all flesh; and the waters shall no more become a flood to destroy all flesh.

GENESIS 9:12-15

To every thing there is a season, and a time to every purpose under the heaven: A time to be born, and a time to die; a time to plant, and a time to pluck up that which is planted; A time to kill, and a time to heal; a time to break down, and a time to build up; A time to weep, and a time to laugh; a time to mourn, and a time to dance; A time to cast away stones, and a time to gather stones together; a time to embrace, and a time to refrain from embracing; A time to get, and a time to lose; a time to keep, and a time to cast away; A time to rend, and a time to sew; a time to keep silence, and a time to speak; A time to love, and a time to hate; a time of war, and a time of peace. He hath made every thing beautiful in his time: also he hath set the world in their heart, so that no man can find out the work that God maketh from the beginning to the end.

ECCLESIASTES 3:1-8, 11

The city of Capernaum, pictured above, is known today as Tell Hum, Israel. Located on the northern coast of the Sea of Galilee, Capernaum, a central point for Jesus' ministry, was where He miraculously healed the loved ones of many believers, including the centurion's servant, Peter's mother-in-law, and the son of a nobleman. (Photograph by Stockman/International Stock)

JOY AND PRAISE

Make a joyful noise unto the LORD, all ye lands. Serve the LORD with gladness: come before his presence with singing.

PSALM 100:1, 2

O LORD our Lord, how excellent is thy name in all the earth! who hast set thy glory above the heavens. When I consider thy heavens, the work of thy fingers, the moon and the stars, which thou hast ordained; What is man, that thou art mindful of him? and the son of man, that thou visitest him? For thou hast made him a little lower than the angels, and hast crowned him with glory and honour. O LORD our Lord, how excellent is thy name in all the earth!

PSALM 8:1, 3-5, 9

And the disciples went, and did as Jesus commanded them, And brought the ass, and the colt, and put on them their clothes, and they set him thereon. And a very great multitude spread their garments in the way; others cut down branches from the trees, and strawed them in the way. And the multitudes that went before, and that followed, cried, saying, Hosanna to the son of David: Blessed is he that cometh in the name of the Lord; Hosanna in the highest. And when he was come into Jerusalem, all the city was moved, saying, Who is this? And the multitude said, This is Jesus the prophet of Nazareth of Galilee.

MATTHEW 21:6-11

The scene above is in Jaffa, a part of Tel Aviv, Israel. In Biblical times this area was known as Joppa and was an important seaport that provided access to the Mediterranean for land-locked Jerusalem. (Photograph by Stockman/International Stock)

Sing unto the LORD; for he hath done excellent things: this is known in all the earth.

Isaiah 12:5

I delight to do thy will, O my God: yea, thy law is within my heart.

Psalm 40:8

I was glad when they said unto me, Let us go into the house of the LORD.

Psalm 122:1

This is the day which the LORD hath made; we will rejoice and be glad in it.

Psalm 118:24

For ye shall go out with joy, and be led forth with peace: the mountains and the hills shall break forth before you into singing, and all the trees of the field shall clap their hands.

Isaiah 55:12

Know ye that the LORD he is God: it is he that hath made us, and not we ourselves; we are his people, and the sheep of his pasture. Enter into his gates with thanksgiving, and into his courts with praise: be thankful unto him, and bless his name. For the LORD is good; his mercy is everlasting; and his truth endureth to all generations.

Psalm 100:3-5

Lord, thou hast been our dwellingplace in all generations. Before the mountains were brought forth, or ever thou hadst formed the earth and the world, even from everlasting to everlasting, thou art God.

Psalm 90:1, 2

O LORD, thou art my God; I will exalt thee, I will praise thy name; for thou hast done wonderful things; thy counsels of old are faithfulness and truth.

Isaiah 25:1

Therefore with joy shall ye draw water out of the wells of salvation. And in that day shall ye say, Praise the LORD, call upon his name, declare his doings among the people, make mention that his name is exalted.

ISAIAH 12:3, 4

Sing praises to God, sing praises: sing praises unto our King, sing praises.

PSALM 47:6

Arise, shine; for thy light is come, and the glory of the LORD is risen upon thee.

ISAIAH 60:1

And Mary said, My soul doth magnify the Lord, And my spirit hath rejoiced in God my Saviour. For he hath regarded the low estate of his handmaiden: for, behold, from henceforth all generations shall call me blessed. For he that is mighty hath done to me great things; and holy is his name.

LUKE 1:46-49

Sing unto the LORD a new song, and his praise from the end of the earth.

ISAIAH 42:10A

And he hath put a new song in my mouth, even praise unto our God: many shall see it, and fear, and shall trust in the LORD.

PSALM 40:35

O sing unto the LORD a new song: sing unto the LORD, all the earth. Sing unto the LORD, bless his name; shew forth his salvation from day to day. Declare his glory among the heathen, his wonders among all people. For the LORD is great, and greatly to be praised: he is to be feared above all gods.

PSALM 96:1-4

Rejoice in the Lord alway: and again I say, Rejoice.

PHILIPPIANS 4:4

The heavens declare the glory of God; and the firmament sheweth his handywork.

PSALM 19:1

Ah Lord GOD! behold, thou hast made the heaven and the earth by thy great power and stretched out arm, and there is nothing too hard for thee: Thou shewest lovingkindness unto thousands, and recompensest the iniquity of the fathers into the bosom of their children after them: the Great, the Mighty God, the LORD of hosts, is his name, Great in counsel, and mighty in work: for thine eyes are open upon all the ways of the sons of men: to give every one according to his ways, and according to the fruit of his doings.

JEREMIAH 32:17-19

Therefore will I offer in his tabernacle sacrifices of joy; I will sing, yea, I will sing praises unto the LORD.

PSALM 27:6B

The Negev (meaning dry or parched), pictured at left, lies in southernmost Israel. In ancient times, this harsh and arid region contained important travel and trade routes to Egypt. During a famine, Abraham journeyed across the Negev to reach the fertile Nile Valley in Egypt. Today, with widespread irrigation, the Negev is a less harsh and more habitable landscape. (Photograph by S. Vidler/Superstock)

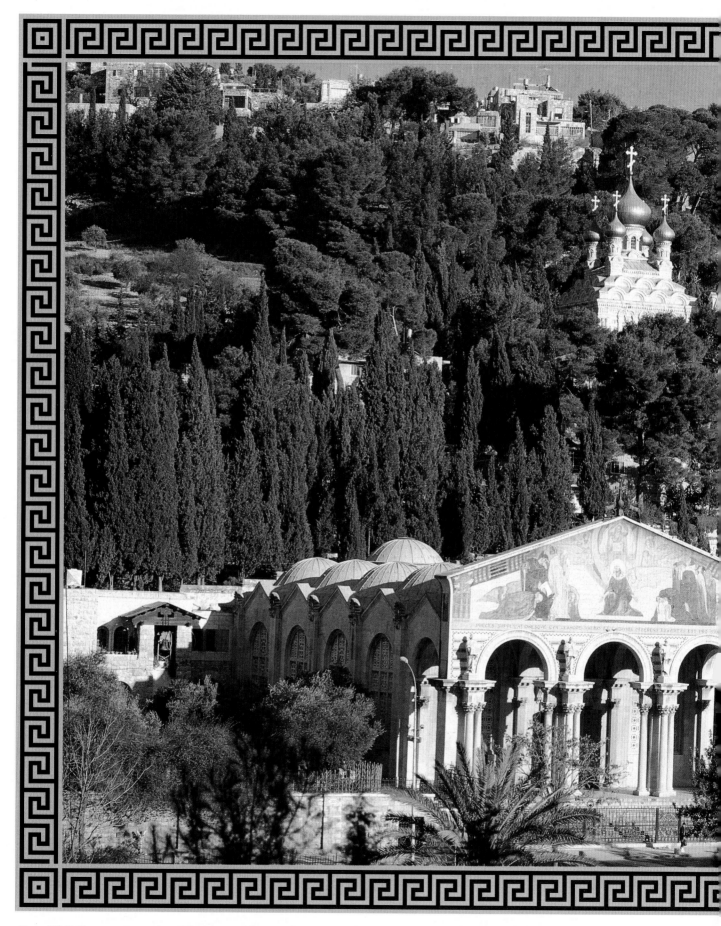

From Biblical accounts, we know that the temple was important to Christ. At age twelve, Jesus amazed Jerusalem's temple leaders with His knowledge; as an adult, He forced the money changers from the temple, which was supposed to be a house of worship. Above are two of Jerusalem's modern houses of worship, the Church of All Nations (foreground) and the Church of Mary Magdalene. (Photograph by Stockman/International Stock)

COMFORT

Let not
your heart
be troubled:
ye believe in God,
believe also in me.
In my Father's house
are many mansions:
if it were not so,
I would have
told you.

JOHN 14:1, 2A

The LORD is my shepherd; I shall not want. He maketh me to lie down in green pastures: he leadeth me beside the still waters. He restoreth my soul: he leadeth me in the paths of righteousness for his name's sake. Yea, though I walk through the valley of the shadow of death, I will fear no evil: for thou art with me; thy rod and thy staff they comfort me. Thou preparest a table before me in the presence of mine enemies: thou anointest my head with oil; my cup runneth over. Surely goodness and mercy shall follow me all the days of my life: and I will dwell in the house of the LORD for ever.

PSALM 23

The image of the Lord as a shepherd and humankind as His sheep is one of the most familiar and comforting in all the Bible. It is not unusual that the Bible is full of sheep and shepherd imagery; throughout Middle Eastern history, sheep have been crucial to the people's livelihood. Here, a flock grazes on Lebanon Mountain near Syria. (Photograph by H. Kanus/Superstock)

It is the same God which worketh all in all.

I CORINTHIANS 12:6B

He shall feed his flock like a shepherd: he shall gather the lambs with his arm, and carry them in his bosom, and shall gently lead those that are with young.

ISAIAH 40:11

I will lift up mine eyes unto the hills, from whence cometh my help. My help cometh from the LORD, which made heaven and earth. He will not suffer thy foot to be moved: he that keepeth thee will not slumber.

PSALM 121:1-3

O God, thou art my God; early will I seek thee: my soul thirsteth for thee, my flesh longeth for thee in a dry and thirsty land, where no water is.

PSALM 63:1

Incline your ear, and come unto me: hear, and your soul shall live; and I will make an everlasting covenant with you, even the sure mercies of David.

ISAIAH 55:3

Comfort ye, comfort ye my people, saith your God.

ISAIAH 40:1

My sheep hear my voice, and I know them, and they follow me: And I give unto them eternal life; and they shall never perish, neither shall any man pluck them out of my hand. My Father, which gave them me, is greater than all; and no man is able to pluck them out of my Father's hand. I and my Father are one.

JOHN 10:27-30

Come unto me, all ye that labour and are heavy laden, and I will give you rest. Take my yoke upon you, and learn of me; for I am meek and lowly in heart: and ye shall find rest unto your souls. For my yoke is easy, and my burden is light.

MATTHEW 11:28-30

I am the good shepherd, and know my sheep, and am known of mine. As the Father knoweth me, even so know I the Father: and I lay down my life for the sheep.

JOHN 10:14, 15

How think ye? if a man have an hundred sheep, and one of them be gone astray, doth he not leave the ninety and nine, and goeth into the mountains, and seeketh that which is gone astray? And if so be that he find it, verily I say unto you, he rejoiceth more of that sheep, than of the ninety and nine which went not astray.

MATTHEW 18:12, 13

I will go before thee, and make the crooked places straight: I will break in pieces the gates of brass, and cut in sunder the bars of iron: And I will give thee the treasures of darkness, and hidden riches of secret places, that thou mayest know that I, the LORD, which call thee by thy name, am the God of Israel.

ISAIAH 45:2, 3

I go to prepare a place for you. And if I go and prepare a place for you, I will come again, and receive you unto myself; that where I am, there ye may be also. And whither I go ye know, and the way ye know.

JOHN 14:2B-4

Jesus' Sermon on the Mount, recorded in Matthew 5-7, was most likely delivered from what we know as the Mount of the Beatitudes, a small slope on the shore of the Sea of Galilee. Jesus' words are a moving and eloquent description of the Christian way of life. Pictured here is the church built on the site in Israel where scholars believe the great sermon was delivered. (Photograph by Buddy Mays/International Stock)

Blessed are the poor in spirit: for theirs is the kingdom of heaven. Blessed are they that mourn: for they shall be comforted. Blessed are the meek: for they shall inherit the earth. Blessed are they which do hunger and thirst after righteousness: for they shall be filled. Blessed are the merciful: for they shall obtain mercy. Blessed are the pure in heart: for they shall see God. Blessed are the peacemakers: for they shall be called the children of God. Blessed are they which are persecuted for righteousness' sake: for theirs is the kingdom of heaven. Blessed are ye, when men shall revile you, and persecute you, and shall say all manner of evil against you falsely, for my sake. Rejoice, and be exceeding glad: for great is your reward in heaven: for so persecuted they the prophets which were before you.

MATTHEW 5:3-12

At least seven of Jesus' disciples made their living by fishing, which was a major industry in Biblical times. The artist's work above is found at the church at Tabgha in Israel, which is believed to be located at the spot where Jesus multiplied the fish and loaves to feed the crowd of thousands (John 6:1-14). (Photograph by Buddy Mays/International Stock)

If ye love me, keep my commandments. And I will pray the Father, and he shall give you another Comforter, that he may abide with you for ever; Even the Spirit of truth; whom the world cannot receive, because it seeth him not, neither knoweth him: but ye know him; for he dwelleth with you, and shall be in you. I will not leave you comfortless: I will come to you. Yet a little while, and the world seeth me no more; but ye see me: because I live, ye shall live also. At that day ye shall know that I am in my Father, and ye in me, and I in you.

JOHN 14:15-20

Pictured here is Nimrod's Fortress which is located within the present-day Golan Heights. The Golan Heights lie northeast of the Sea of Galilee in the territory that borders the countries of Lebanon, Syria, and Jordan. The area takes its name from the ancient city of Golan, which was located east of the Jordan River in the nation of Bashan. (Photograph by Superstock)

COURAGE

I can do
all things
through Christ
which
strengtheneth
me.

PHILIPPIANS 4:13

And when they were departed, behold, the angel of the Lord appeareth to Joseph in a dream, saying, Arise, and take the young child and his mother, and flee into Egypt, and be thou there until I bring thee word: for Herod will seek the young child to destroy him. When he arose, he took the young child and his mother by night, and departed into Egypt. But when Herod was dead, behold, an angel of the Lord appeareth in a dream to Joseph in Egypt, Saying, Arise, and take the young child and his mother, and go into the land of Israel: for they are dead which sought the young child's life.

MATTHEW 2:13, 14, 19, 20

When Joseph fled with the infant Jesus to Egypt, he was returning to a land that his forefathers inhabited for over four hundred years before Moses led them out of Egyptian captivity through the wilderness and into Canaan. The camel and the pyramid, pictured above, are two of the most enduring symbols of the ancient nation of Egypt. (Photograph by S. Vidler/Superstock)

And we know that all things work together for good to them that love God, to them who are the called according to his purpose. For whom he did foreknow, he also did predestinate to be conformed to the image of his Son, that he might be the firstborn among many brethren. Moreover whom he did predestinate, them he also called: and whom he called, them he also justified: and whom he justified, them he also glorified. What shall we then say to these things? If God be for us, who can be against us? He that spared not his own Son, but delivered him up for us all, how shall he not with him also freely give us all things?

ROMANS 8:28-32

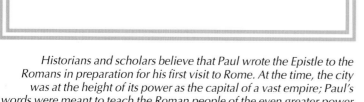

Historians and scholars believe that Paul wrote the Epistle to the Romans in preparation for his first visit to Rome. At the time, the city was at the height of its power as the capital of a vast empire; Paul's words were meant to teach the Roman people of the even greater power of God's love. Pictured at right are the ruins of the Roman Forum, once a center of Roman activity. (Photograph by G. Barone/Superstock)

I have set the LORD always before me: because he is at my right hand, I shall not be moved.

PSALM 16:8

And Jesus looking upon them saith, With men it is impossible, but not with God: for with God all things are possible.

MARK 10:27

Fear thou not; for I am with thee: be not dismayed; for I am thy God: I will strengthen thee; yea, I will help thee; yea, I will uphold thee with the right hand of my righteousness.

ISAIAH 41:10

For I the LORD thy God will hold thy right hand, saying unto thee, Fear not; I will help thee.

ISAIAH 41:13

The LORD is my strength and my shield; my heart trusted in him, and I am helped: therefore my heart greatly rejoiceth; and with my song will I praise him.

PSALM 28:7

Behold, God is my salvation; I will trust, and not be afraid: for the LORD JEHOVAH is my strength and my song; he also is become my salvation.

ISAIAH 12:2

And he said unto me, My grace is sufficient for thee: for my strength is made perfect in weakness. Most gladly therefore will I rather glory in my infirmities, that the power of Christ may rest upon me.

II CORINTHIANS 12:9

God is our refuge and strength, a very present help in trouble. Therefore will not we fear; though the earth be removed, and though the mountains be carried into the midst of the sea.

PSALM 46:1, 2

Be strong and of a good courage, fear not, nor be afraid of them: for the LORD thy God, he it is that doth go with thee; he will not fail thee, nor forsake thee.

DEUTERONOMY 31:6

Have not I commanded thee? Be strong and of a good courage; be not afraid, neither be thou dismayed: for the LORD thy God is with thee whithersoever thou goest.

JOSHUA 1:9

I will love thee, O LORD, my strength. The LORD is my rock, and my fortress, and my deliverer; my God, my strength, in whom I will trust; my buckler; and the horn of my salvation, and my high tower.

PSALM 18:1, 2

The LORD is my light and my salvation; whom shall I fear? the LORD is the strength of my life; of whom shall I be afraid?

PSALM 27:1

Hast thou not known? hast thou not heard, that the everlasting God, the LORD, the Creator of the ends of the earth, fainteth not, neither is weary? there is no searching of his understanding. He giveth power to the faint; and to them that have no might he increaseth strength. Even the youths shall faint and be weary, and the young men shall utterly fall: But they that wait upon the LORD shall renew their strength; they shall mount up with wings as eagles; they shall run, and not be weary; and they shall walk, and not faint.

ISAIAH 40:28-31

At left are the ruins of a castle in the Biblical city of Byblos, which was an important Phoenician seaport on the Mediterranean during the time of King Solomon. Byblos's chief import was papyrus, which was used to make paper; and historians believe that the word bible ultimately arose from the seaport's name. Today Byblos is located twenty-five miles north of Beirut in Lebanon. (Photograph by Superstock)

The ancient city of Petra was once called the "red-rose city" because of its red sandstone cliffs, which were used for protection by the city's New Testament inhabitants. The archaeological ruins of ancient Petra, pictured above, are found within the borders of modern-day Jordan. (Photograph by Mauritius/Superstock)

VIRTUE AND RIGHTEOUSNESS

Who shall stand in his holy place? He that hath clean hands, and a pure heart.

PSALM 24:3B, 4A

God gave the Ten Commandments to His people at Mt. Sinai through Moses, who had led the Israelites out of Egypt on the road toward Canaan. The Israelites had spent generations in captivity in Egypt, a polytheistic land where great pyramids, like these at Giza, stood to honor royal leaders. (Photograph by M. Howell/Superstock)

And God spake all these words, saying, I am the LORD thy God, which have brought thee out of the land of Egypt, out of the house of bondage. Thou shalt have no other gods before me. Thou shalt not make unto thee any graven image, or any likeness of any thing that is in heaven above, or that is in the earth beneath, or that is in the water under the earth: Thou shalt not bow down thyself to them, nor serve them: for I the LORD thy God am a jealous God, visiting the iniquity of the fathers upon the children unto the third and fourth generation of them that hate me; And shewing mercy unto thousands of them that love me, and keep my commandments.

Thou shalt not take the name of the LORD thy God in vain; for the LORD will not hold him guiltless that taketh his name in vain. Remember the sabbath day, to keep it holy. Six days shalt thou labour, and do all thy work: But the seventh day is the sabbath of the LORD thy God: in it thou shalt not do any work, thou, nor thy son, nor thy daughter, thy manservant, nor thy maidservant, nor thy cattle, nor thy stranger that is within thy gates: For in six days the LORD made heaven and earth, the sea, and all that in them is, and rested the seventh day: wherefore the LORD blessed the sabbath day, and hallowed it.

Honour thy father and thy mother: that thy days may be long upon the land which the LORD thy God giveth thee. Thou shalt not kill. Thou shalt not commit adultery. Thou shalt not steal. Thou shalt not bear false witness against thy neighbour. Thou shalt not covet thy neighbour's house, thou shalt not covet thy neighbour's wife, nor his manservant, nor his maidservant, nor his ox, nor his ass, nor any thing that is thy neighbour's. And all the people saw the thunderings, and the lightnings, and the noise of the trumpet, and the mountain smoking: and when the people saw it, they removed, and stood afar off.

EXODUS 20:1-18

For we wrestle not against flesh and blood, but against principalities, against powers, against the rulers of the darkness of this world, against spiritual wickedness in high places.

EPHESIANS 6:12

For the perfecting of the saints, for the work of the ministry, for the edifying of the body of Christ: Till we all come in the unity of the faith, and of the knowledge of the Son of God, unto a perfect man, unto the measure of the stature of the fulness of Christ.

EPHESIANS 4:12, 13

And when the tempter came to him, he said, If thou be the Son of God, command that these stones be made bread. But he answered and said, It is written, Man shall not live by bread alone, but by every word that proceedeth out of the mouth of God.

MATTHEW 4:3, 4

But as he which hath called you is holy, so be ye holy in all manner of conversation; Because it is written, Be ye holy; for I am holy.

I PETER 1:15, 16

He that loveth father or mother more than me is not worthy of me: and he that loveth son or daughter more than me is not worthy of me. And he that taketh not his cross, and followeth after me, is not worthy of me. He that findeth his life shall lose it: and he that loseth his life for my sake shall find it.

MATTHEW 10:37-39

Ye are the light of the world. A city that is set on an hill cannot be hid. Neither do men light a candle, and put it under a bushel, but on a candlestick; and it giveth light unto all that are in the house. Let your light so shine before men, that they may see your good works, and glorify your Father which is in heaven.

MATTHEW 5:14-16

As he spake these words, many believed on him. Then said Jesus to those Jews which believed on him, If ye continue in my word, then are ye my disciples indeed.

JOHN 8:30, 31

Draw nigh to God, and he will draw nigh to you. Cleanse your hands, ye sinners; and purify your hearts, ye double minded.

JAMES 4:8

Enter ye in at the strait gate: for wide is the gate, and broad is the way, that leadeth to destruction, and many there be which go in thereat: Because strait is the gate, and narrow is the way, which leadeth unto life, and few there be that find it.

MATTHEW 7:13, 14

But be ye doers of the word, and not hearers only, deceiving your own selves.

JAMES 1:22

What? know ye not that your body is the temple of the Holy Ghost which is in you, which ye have of God, and ye are not your own? For ye are bought with a price: therefore glorify God in your body, and in your spirit, which are God's.

I CORINTHIANS 6:19, 20

He maketh his sun to rise on the evil and on the good, and sendeth rain on the just and on the unjust. For if ye love them which love you, what reward have ye? do not even the publicans the same? And if ye salute your brethren only, what do ye more than others? do not even the publicans so? Be ye therefore perfect, even as your Father which is in heaven is perfect.

MATTHEW 5:45B-48

I beseech you therefore, brethren, by the mercies of God, that ye present your bodies a living sacrifice, holy, acceptable unto God, which is your reasonable service. And be not conformed to this world: but be ye transformed by the renewing of your mind, that ye may prove what is that good, and acceptable, and perfect, will of God. For I say, through the grace given unto me, to every man that is among you, not to think of himself more highly than he ought to think; but to think soberly, according as God hath dealt to every man the measure of faith.

For as we have many members in one body, and all members have not the same office: So we, being many, are one body in Christ, and every one members one of another. Having then gifts differing according to the grace that is given to us, whether prophecy, let us prophesy according to the proportion of faith; Or ministry, let us wait on our ministering: or he that teacheth, on teaching; Or he that exhorteth, on exhortation: he that giveth, let him do it with simplicity; he that ruleth, with diligence; he that sheweth mercy, with cheerfulness. Let love be without dissimulation. Abhor that which is evil; cleave to that which is good. Be kindly affectioned one to another with brotherly love; in honour preferring one another; Not slothful in business; fervent in spirit; serving the Lord; Rejoicing in hope; patient in tribulation; continuing instant in prayer; Distributing to the necessity of saints; given to hospitality.

Bless them which persecute you: bless, and curse not. Rejoice with them that do rejoice, and weep with them that weep. Be of the same mind one toward another. Mind not high things, but condescend to men of low estate. Be not wise in your own conceits. Recompense to no man evil for evil. Provide things honest in the sight of all men.

ROMANS 12:1-17

The nation of Syria has existed for thousands of years. In Biblical times, the Syrians were often at war with Israel, and their land was used as a corridor for armies invading Palestine. This long and tumultous history has made Syria a prime spot for modern achaeological studies. The ruins of the ancient castle at right are located at Homs Sytia in modern-day Syria. (Photograph by H. Kanus/Superstock)

The description of the "virtuous woman" at right is
taken from the final chapter of the Book of Proverbs,
which praises the wise, hardworking woman.
Above, young, modern-day Bedouin women tend
to their goats in Israel. (Photograph by S.
Vidler/Superstock)

Who can find a virtuous woman? for her price is far above rubies. The heart of her husband doth safely trust in her, so that he shall have no need of spoil. She will do him good and not evil all the days of her life. She seeketh wool, and flax, and worketh willingly with her hands. She is like the merchants' ships; she bringeth her food from afar. She riseth also while it is yet night, and giveth meat to her household, and a portion to her maidens.

She considereth a field, and buyeth it: with the fruit of her hands she planteth a vineyard. She girdeth her loins with strength, and strengtheneth her arms. She perceiveth that her merchandise is good: her candle goeth not out by night. She layeth her hands to the spindle, and her hands hold the distaff. She stretcheth out her hand to the poor; yea, she reacheth forth her hands to the needy. She is not afraid of the snow for her household: for all her household are clothed with scarlet. She maketh herself coverings of tapestry; her clothing is silk and purple.

Her husband is known in the gates, when he sitteth among the elders of the land. She maketh fine linen, and selleth it; and delivereth girdles unto the merchant. Strength and honour are her clothing; and she shall rejoice in time to come. She openeth her mouth with wisdom; and in her tongue is the law of kindness. She looketh well to the ways of her household, and eateth not the bread of idleness. Her children arise up, and call her blessed; her husband also, and he praiseth her. Many daughters have done virtuously, but thou excellest them all.

Favour is deceitful, and beauty is vain: but a woman that feareth the LORD, she shall be praised. Give her of the fruit of her hands; and let her own works praise her in the gates.

PROVERBS 31:10-31

Blessed is the man that walketh not in the counsel of the ungodly, nor standeth in the way of sinners, nor sitteth in the seat of the scornful. But his delight is in the law of the LORD; and in his law doth he meditate day and night.

PSALM 1:1, 2

And Jesus answered and said unto him, Get thee behind me, Satan: for it is written, Thou shalt worship the Lord thy God, and him only shalt thou serve.

LUKE 4:8

And if a house be divided against itself, that house cannot stand.

MARK 3:25

As it is written, There is none righteous, no, not one: There is none that understandeth, there is none that seeketh after God.

ROMANS 3:10, 11

It is easier for a camel to go through the eye of a needle, than for a rich man to enter into the kingdom of God.

MARK 10:25

Rejoice evermore. Pray without ceasing. In every thing give thanks: for this is the will of God in Christ Jesus concerning you. Quench not the Spirit. Despise not prophesyings. Prove all things; hold fast that which is good. Abstain from all appearance of evil. And the very God of peace sanctify you wholly; and I pray God your whole spirit and soul and body be preserved blameless unto the coming of our Lord Jesus Christ. Faithful is he that calleth you, who also will do it. Brethren, pray for us. Greet all the brethren with an holy kiss. I charge you by the Lord that this epistle be read unto all the holy brethren. The grace of our Lord Jesus Christ be with you. Amen.

I THESSALONIANS 5:16-28

Choose you this day whom ye will serve; whether the gods which your fathers served that were on the other side of the flood, or the gods of the Amorites, in whose land ye dwell: but as for me and my house, we will serve the LORD.

JOSHUA 24:15B

That all men should honour the Son, even as they honour the Father. He that honoureth not the Son honoureth not the Father which hath sent him.

JOHN 5:23

Be not deceived; God is not mocked: for whatsoever a man soweth, that shall he also reap. For he that soweth to his flesh shall of the flesh reap corruption; but he that soweth to the Spirit shall of the Spirit reap life everlasting.

GALATIANS 6:7, 8

His lord said unto him, Well done, thou good and faithful servant: thou hast been faithful over a few things, I will make thee ruler over many things: enter thou into the joy of thy lord.

MATTHEW 25:21

But the fruit of the Spirit is love, joy, peace, long-suffering, gentleness, goodness, faith, Meekness, temperance: against such there is no law. And they that are Christ's have crucified the flesh with the affections and lusts. If we live in the Spirit, let us also walk in the Spirit.

GALATIANS 5:22-25

And if thy right eye offend thee, pluck it out, and cast it from thee: for it is profitable for thee that one of thy members should perish, and not that thy whole body should be cast into hell.

MATTHEW 5:29

For centuries, Greek language and culture dominated much of the known world. Even after the Romans conquered Greece in 146 B.C., Greece continued to have far-reaching influence; in fact, the majority of the original New Testament text is in Greek. Pictured above is Milos, part of the Cyclades Islands in Greece. (Photograph by P. Cantor/Superstock)

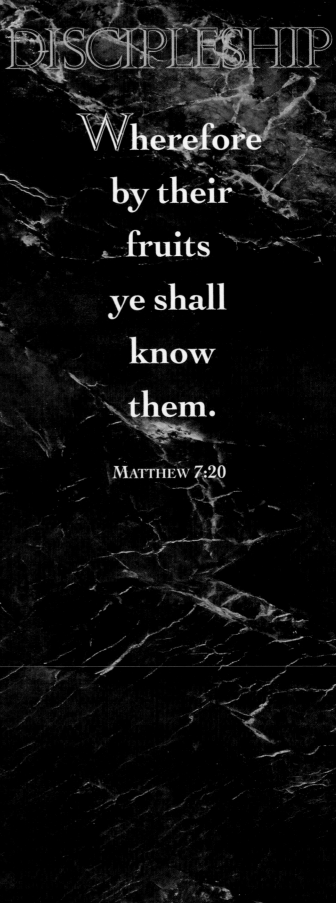

DISCIPLESHIP

Wherefore by their fruits ye shall know them.

MATTHEW 7:20

*Pictured above is the countryside of Iraq, the modern
nation that occupies most of the land once known as
Mesopotamia, generally believed to have been the land
between the Tigris and Euphrates Rivers. Abraham was
born in the city of Ur in southern Mesopotamia. (Photograph by S. Fiore/Superstock)*

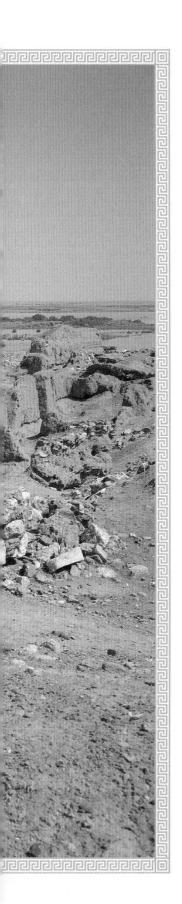

I am the true vine, and my Father is the husbandman. Every branch in me that beareth not fruit he taketh away: and every branch that beareth fruit, he purgeth it, that it may bring forth more fruit. Now ye are clean through the word which I have spoken unto you. Abide in me, and I in you. As the branch cannot bear fruit of itself, except it abide in the vine; no more can ye, except ye abide in me. I am the vine, ye are the branches: He that abideth in me, and I in him, the same bringeth forth much fruit: for without me ye can do nothing. If a man abide not in me, he is cast forth as a branch, and is withered; and men gather them, and cast them into the fire, and they are burned. If ye abide in me, and my words abide in you, ye shall ask what ye will, and it shall be done unto you. Herein is my Father glorified, that ye bear much fruit; so shall ye be my disciples. As the Father hath loved me, so have I loved you: continue ye in my love.

JOHN 15:1-9

*And he said unto them,
Go ye into all the world,
and preach the gospel to
every creature.*

MARK 16:15

*And he saith unto them,
Follow me, and I will make you fishers of
men. And they straightway left their nets,
and followed him.*

MATTHEW 4:19, 20

*And these words, which I command thee this day, shall be in thine heart: And thou
shalt teach them diligently unto thy children, and shalt talk of them when thou sittest
in thine house, and when thou walkest by the way, and when thou liest down, and when
thou risest up. And thou shalt bind them for a sign upon thine hand, and they shall be
as frontlets between thine eyes. And thou shalt write them upon the posts of thy house,
and on thy gates.*

DEUTERONOMY 6:6-9

*Now the God of patience and con-
solation grant you to be like-
minded one toward another
according to Christ Jesus: That
ye may with one mind and one
mouth glorify God, even the
Father of our Lord Jesus Christ.
Wherefore receive ye one another,
as Christ also received us to the
glory of God.*

ROMANS 15:5-7

*And he said unto them, It is not for
you to know the times or the seasons,
which the Father hath put in his own
power. But ye shall receive power,
after that the Holy Ghost is come
upon you: and ye shall be witnesses
unto me both in Jerusalem, and in all
Judaea, and in Samaria, and unto
the uttermost part of the earth.*

ACTS 1:7, 8

And Jesus came and spake unto them, saying, All power is given unto me in heaven and in earth. Go ye therefore, and teach all nations, baptizing them in the name of the Father, and of the Son, and of the Holy Ghost: Teaching them to observe all things whatsoever I have commanded you: and, lo, I am with you alway, even unto the end of the world. Amen.

MATTHEW 28:18-20

Then saith he unto his disciples, The harvest truly is plenteous, but the labourers are few; Pray ye therefore the Lord of the harvest, that he will send forth labourers into his harvest.

MATTHEW 9:37, 38

And the gospel must first be published among all nations.

MARK 13:10

For whosoever shall call upon the name of the Lord shall be saved. How then shall they call on him in whom they have not believed? and how shall they believe in him of whom they have not heard? and how shall they hear without a preacher? And how shall they preach, except they be sent? as it is written, How beautiful are the feet of them that preach the gospel of peace, and bring glad tidings of good things!

ROMANS 10:13-15

How beautiful upon the mountains are the feet of him that bringeth good tidings, that publisheth peace; that bringeth good tidings of good, that publisheth salvation; that saith unto Zion, Thy God reigneth!

ISAIAH 52:7

And when the day of Pentecost was fully come, they were all with one accord in one place. And suddenly there came a sound from heaven as of a rushing mighty wind, and it filled all the house where they were sitting. And there appeared unto them cloven tongues like as of fire, and it sat upon each of them. And they were all filled with the Holy Ghost, and began to speak with other tongues, as the Spirit gave them utterance.

ACTS 2:1-4

Above, women in modern-day Iraq make sun-dried clay bricks. Working with clay to make bricks or pottery is a tradition that dates back further than written history; the first known potter's wheel was developed more than three thousand years before Christ's birth. Several Biblical passages use pottery making to symbolize God's relationship to man.
(Photograph by Superstock)

In Old Testament times, the present-day city of Dhiban, Jordan, pictured above, was the Moabite city of Dibon, home to Mesha, the king of Moab. Mesha recorded the details of his revolt against Israel on a large slab of stone which, in 1868, was discovered by a German missionary. (Photograph by H. Kanus/Superstock)

KINDNESS

A soft answer
turneth away
wrath: but
grievous
words stir
up anger.

PROVERBS 15:1

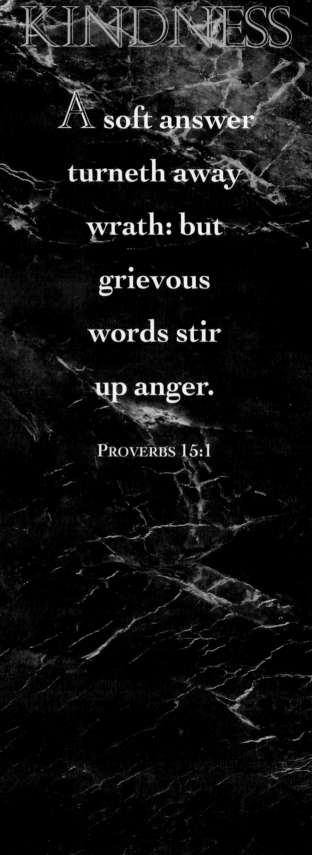

But when Jesus saw it, he . . . said unto them, Suffer the little children to come unto me, and forbid them not: for of such is the kingdom of God. Verily I say unto you, Whosoever shall not receive the kingdom of God as a little child, he shall not enter therein. And he took them up in his arms, put his hands upon them, and blessed them.

MARK 10:14-16

He that receiveth you receiveth me, and he that receiveth me receiveth him that sent me. He that receiveth a prophet in the name of a prophet shall receive a prophet's reward; and he that receiveth a righteous man in the name of a righteous man shall receive a righteous man's reward. And whosoever shall give to drink unto one of these little ones a cup of cold water only in the name of a disciple, verily I say unto you, he shall in no wise lose his reward.

MATTHEW 10:40-42

Then one of them, which was a lawyer, asked him a question, tempting him, and saying, Master, which is the great commandment in the law? Jesus said unto him, Thou shalt love the Lord thy God with all thy heart, and with all thy soul, and with all thy mind. This is the first and great commandment. And the second is like unto it, Thou shalt love thy neighbour as thyself. On these two commandments hang all the law and the prophets.

MATTHEW 22:35-40

The Sea of Galilee, actually a freshwater lake fed by the Jordan River, is located about sixty miles north of Jerusalem. Called the Sea of Chinnereth, the Lake of Gennesaret, and the Sea of Tiberias in addition to its more familiar name, the Sea of Galilee (pictured above) was the site of most of Jesus' miracles and much of His preaching. (Photograph by J. G. Edmanson/International Stock)

Pictured above is the tomb of Zachariah in the Kidron Valley.
The valley, carved by a seasonal brook that runs eastward to
the Dead Sea, defines the eastern edge of Jerusalem. Jesus, on
the night of His betrayal, crossed the Kidron Brook, then
named Cedron, on His way to the Garden of Gethsemane.
(Photograph by Superstock)

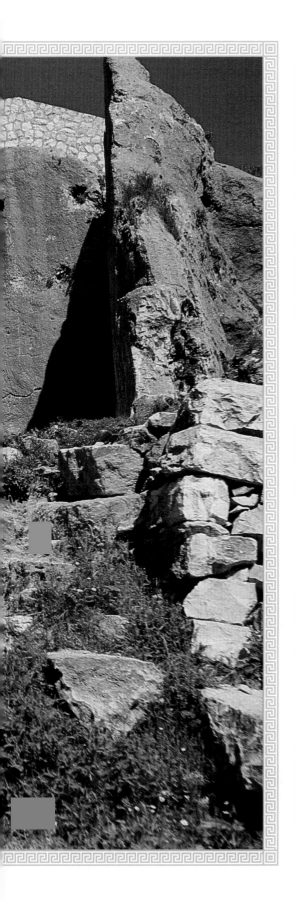

For I was an hungred, and ye gave me meat: I was thirsty, and ye gave me drink: I was a stranger, and ye took me in: Naked, and ye clothed me: I was sick, and ye visited me: I was in prison, and ye came unto me. Then shall the righteous answer him, saying, Lord, when saw we thee an hungred, and fed thee? or thirsty, and gave thee drink? When saw we thee a stranger, and took thee in? or naked, and clothed thee? Or when saw we thee sick, or in prison, and came unto thee? And the King shall answer and say unto them, Verily I say unto you, Inasmuch as ye have done it unto one of the least of these my brethren, ye have done it unto me.

MATTHEW 25:35-40

Take heed that ye despise not one of these little ones; for I say unto you, That in heaven their angels do always behold the face of my Father which is in heaven.

MATTHEW 18:10

Ye have heard that it hath been said, An eye for an eye, and a tooth for a tooth: But I say unto you, That ye resist not evil: but whosoever shall smite thee on thy right cheek, turn to him the other also. And if any man will sue thee at the law, and take away thy coat, let him have thy cloak also. And whosoever shall compel thee to go a mile, go with him twain. Give to him that asketh thee, and from him that would borrow of thee turn not thou away.

MATTHEW 5:38-42

And be ye kind one to another, tenderhearted, forgiving one another, even as God for Christ's sake hath forgiven you. Be ye therefore followers of God as dear children.

EPHESIANS 4:32; 5:1

Pleasant words are as an honeycomb, sweet to the soul, and health to the bones.

PROVERBS 16:24

The church at left in Tabgha, Israel, commemorates Jesus' miracle of the loaves and fish. On a mountain beside the Sea of Galilee, Jesus fed thousands of followers with "five barley loaves, and two small fishes" (John 6:9). His actions made true believers out of all present. (Photograph by Buddy Mays/International Stock)

Pictured here are the ruins at Santorini, Greece. By the time of Jesus' birth, the great Greek Empire that had dominated the ancient world had been overtaken by the Romans. Nonetheless, Greek culture and language proved too powerful a force for the Romans to overcome, and the influence of the Greek Empire continued to shape everyday life throughout the ancient world. (Photograph by G. Outerbridge/Superstock)

LOVE

Greater love
hath no
man than this,
that a man
lay down
his life for
his friends.

JOHN 15:13

And they lifted up their voice, and wept again: and Orpah kissed her mother in law; but Ruth clave unto her. And she said, Behold, thy sister in law is gone back unto her people, and unto her gods: return thou after thy sister in law. And Ruth said, Intreat me not to leave thee, or to return from following after thee: for whither thou goest, I will go; and where thou lodgest, I will lodge: thy people shall be my people, and thy God my God: Where thou diest, will I die, and there will I be buried: the LORD do so to me, and more also, if aught but death part thee and me. When she saw that she was stedfastly minded to go with her, then she left speaking unto her. So they two went until they came to Bethlehem.

RUTH 1:14-19A

Beloved, let us love one another: for love is of God; and every one that loveth is born of God, and knoweth God. He that loveth not knoweth not God; for God is love.

I JOHN 4:7, 8

According to tradition, the high fortress of Masada, pictured above, which lies south of Jerusalem, was the site of a courageous resistance by a small group of Jews who refused to surrender after the Romans invaded Jerusalem in A.D. 73. The Jewish free-dom fighters, who would not renounce their God and accept Roman religious beliefs, made a valiant stand against the invaders at Masada before finally commit-ting suicide to avoid capture. (Photograph by A. Friedlander/Superstock)

Again, a new commandment I write unto you, which thing is true in him and in you: because the darkness is past, and the true light now shineth. He that saith he is in the light, and hateth his brother, is in darkness even until now. He that loveth his brother abideth in the light, and there is none occasion of stumbling in him. But he that hateth his brother is in darkness, and walketh in darkness, and knoweth not whither he goeth, because that darkness hath blinded his eyes. I write unto you, little children, because your sins are forgiven you for his name's sake.

I JOHN 2:8-12

Herein is our love made perfect, that we may have boldness in the day of judgment: because as he is, so are we in this world. There is no fear in love; but perfect love casteth out fear: because fear hath torment. He that feareth is not made perfect in love. We love him, because he first loved us. If a man say, I love God, and hateth his brother, he is a liar: for he that loveth not his brother whom he hath seen, how can he love God whom he hath not seen? And this commandment have we from him, That he who loveth God love his brother also.

I JOHN 4:17-21

The Apostle John (John 5:5) tells the story of a man, lame for thirty-eight years, who journeyed to the pool of Bethesda in northeastern Jerusalem to be healed. Scholars believe that the small pool is one of the two pictured here. Although the lame man made the journey because he believed in the power of the waters, he was, instead, healed by the grace of God through the intervention of Jesus. (Photograph by Jeff Greenberg/International Stock)

*Love not the world, neither the
things that are in the world. If
any man love the world, the love
of the Father
is not in him.*

I JOHN 2:15

*And walk in love,
as Christ also hath loved us,
and hath given himself for us
an offering and a sacrifice to God for a
sweetsmelling savour.*

EPHESIANS 5:2

*Two are better than one;
because they have a good reward
for their labour.
For if they fall,
the one will lift up his fellow:
but woe to him that is
alone when he falleth;
for he hath not another
to help him up.
Again, if two lie together,
then they have heat:
but how can one be warm alone?
And if one prevail against him,
two shall withstand him;
and a threefold cord is not
quickly broken.*

ECCLESIASTES 4:9-12

*My beloved spake, and said unto me,
Rise up, my love, my fair one,
and come away. For, lo, the winter is
past, the rain is over and gone;
The flowers appear on the earth;
the time of the singing of birds is come,
and the voice of the turtle
is heard in our land.*

SONG OF SOLOMON 2:10-12

*And hereby we do know that we know
him, if we keep his commandments.
He that saith, I know him, and
keepeth not his commandments, is a
liar, and the truth is not in him. But
whoso keepeth his word, in him verily
is the love of God perfected: hereby
know we that we are in him.*

I JOHN 2:3-5

A friend loveth at all times.

PROVERBS 17:17a

*For this is the love of God,
that we keep his commandments:
and his commandments are not
grievous. For whatsoever is born of
God overcometh the world:
and this is the victory
that overcometh the world,
even our faith.*

I JOHN 5:3, 4

*Therefore, when he was gone out,
Jesus said, Now is the Son of man
glorified, and God is glorified in
him. If God be glorified in him,
God shall also glorify him in himself, and shall straightway glorify
him. Little children, yet a little while
I am with you. Ye shall seek me:
and as I said unto the Jews,
Whither I go, ye cannot come; so
now I say to you. A new
commandment I give unto you, That
ye love one another; as I have loved
you, that ye also love one another.
By this shall all men know that ye
are my disciples,
if ye have love one to another.*

JOHN 13:31-35

*In this was manifested the love of
God toward us, because that God
sent his only begotten Son into the
world, that we might live through
him. Herein is love, not that we
loved God, but that he loved us, and
sent his Son to be the propitiation
for our sins. Beloved, if God so
loved us, we ought also to love one
another. No man hath seen God at
any time. If we love one another,
God dwelleth in us, and his love is
perfected in us. Hereby know we
that we dwell in him, and he in us,
because he hath given us
of his Spirit.*

I JOHN 4:9-13

*These things I command you, that
ye love one another.*

JOHN 15:17

*I love them that love me; and those
that seek me early shall find me.*

PROVERBS 8:17

*Above are the ruins of the Greek Temple of Apollo in Corinth.
Corinth was a vital trade city in ancient Greece and at times
rivaled Athens as the center of Greek wealth and prosperity. The
Apostle Paul came to Corinth—a city with more than half a mil-
lion inhabitants and a reputation for godlessness and immoral-
ity—and founded a church in A.D. 51. (Photograph by Superstock)*

Though I speak with the tongues of men and of angels, and have not charity, I am become as sounding brass, or a tinkling cymbal. And though I have the gift of prophecy, and understand all mysteries, and all knowledge; and though I have all faith, so that I could remove mountains, and have not charity, I am nothing. And though I bestow all my goods to feed the poor, and though I give my body to be burned, and have not charity, it profiteth me nothing. Charity suffereth long, and is kind; charity envieth not; charity vaunteth not itself, is not puffed up, Doth not behave itself unseemly, seeketh not her own, is not easily provoked, thinketh no evil; Rejoiceth not in iniquity, but rejoiceth in the truth; Beareth all things, believeth all things, hopeth all things, endureth all things. Charity never faileth: but whether there be prophecies, they shall fail; whether there be tongues, they shall cease; whether there be knowledge, it shall vanish away. For we know in part, and we prophesy in part. But when that which is perfect is come, then that which is in part shall be done away. When I was a child, I spake as a child, I understood as a child, I thought as a child: but when I became a man, I put away childish things. For now we see through a glass, darkly; but then face to face: now I know in part; but then shall I know even as also I am known. And now abideth faith, hope, charity, these three; but the greatest of these is charity.

I CORINTHIANS 13

The Golan Heights, pictured above, rise above the Sea of Galilee. Located in the fertile district of Bashan, the Golan Heights are surrounded by deep valleys, which were carved by melting snow rushing toward the lake below. (Photograph by Buddy Mays/International Stock)

FAITH

So then
faith
cometh by
hearing,
and hearing
by the
word of God.

ROMANS 10:17

The temptation of Jesus described in Matthew 4:1-11 is believed to have taken place in the mountains that lie outside the city of Jericho, pictured above. The history of this most ancient of cities, located east of Jerusalem near where the Jordan River meets the Dead Sea, is long and storied. This rich past has drawn archaeologists from all over the world to the large mound where the original Jericho once stood. (Photograph by Buddy Mays/International Stock)

Now faith is the substance of things hoped for, the evidence of things not seen. Through faith we understand that the worlds were framed by the word of God, so that things which are seen were not made of things which do appear.

But without faith it is impossible to please him: for he that cometh to God must believe that he is, and that he is a rewarder of them that diligently seek him.

By faith Noah, being warned of God of things not seen as yet, moved with fear, prepared an ark to the saving of his house; by the which he condemned the world, and became heir of the righteousness which is by faith. By faith Abraham, when he was called to go out into a place which he should after receive for an inheritance, obeyed; and he went out, not knowing whither he went. By faith he sojourned in the land of promise, as in a strange country, dwelling in tabernacles with Isaac and Jacob, the heirs with him of the same promise: For he looked for a city which hath foundations, whose builder and maker is God.

Through faith also Sarah herself received strength to conceive seed, and was delivered of a child when she was past age, because she judged him faithful who had promised. Therefore sprang there even of one, and him as good as dead, so many as the stars of the sky in multitude, and as the sand which is by the sea shore innumerable. These all died in faith, not having received the promises, but having seen them afar off, and were persuaded of them, and embraced them, and confessed that they were strangers and pilgrims on the earth.

HEBREWS 11:1, 3, 6-13

And after eight days again his disciples were within, and Thomas with them: then came Jesus, the doors being shut, and stood in the midst, and said, Peace be unto you. Then saith he to Thomas, Reach hither thy finger, and behold my hands; and reach hither thy hand, and thrust it into my side: and be not faithless, but believing. And Thomas answered and said unto him, My Lord and my God. Jesus saith unto him, Thomas, because thou hast seen me, thou hast believed: blessed are they that have not seen, and yet have believed.

JOHN 20:26-29

And Jesus said unto them, Because of your unbelief: for verily I say unto you, If ye have faith as a grain of mustard seed, ye shall say unto this mountain, Remove hence to yonder place; and it shall remove; and nothing shall be impossible unto you.

MATTHEW 17:20

And Jesus said unto him, Go thy way; thy faith hath made thee whole. And immediately he received his sight, and followed Jesus in the way.

MARK 10:52

And his disciples came to him, and awoke him, saying, Lord, save us: we perish. And he saith unto them, Why are ye fearful, O ye of little faith? Then he arose, and rebuked the winds and the sea; and there was a great calm.

MATTHEW 8:25, 26

And the angel said unto her, Fear not, Mary: for thou hast found favour with God. And, behold, thou shalt conceive in thy womb, and bring forth a son, and shalt call his name JESUS. He shall be great, and shall be called the Son of the Highest: and the Lord God shall give unto him the throne of his father David: And he shall reign over the house of Jacob for ever; and of his kingdom there shall be no end.

LUKE 1:30-33

And Mary said, Behold the handmaid of the Lord; be it unto me according to thy word. And the angel departed from her.

LUKE 1:38

For I am not ashamed of the gospel of Christ: for it is the power of God unto salvation to every one that believeth; to the Jew first, and also to the Greek. For therein is the righteousness of God revealed from faith to faith; as it is written, The just shall live by faith.

ROMANS 1:16, 17

And, behold, a woman, which was diseased . . . twelve years, came behind him, and touched the hem of his garment. For she said within herself, If I may but touch his garment, I shall be whole.

MATTHEW 9:20, 21

And in the sixth month the angel Gabriel was sent from God unto a city of Galilee, named Nazareth, To a virgin espoused to a man whose name was Joseph, of the house of David; and the virgin's name was Mary. And the angel came in unto her, and said, Hail, thou that art highly favoured, the Lord is with thee: blessed art thou among women.

LUKE 1:26-28

Jesus said unto him, If thou canst believe, all things are possible to him that believeth. And straightway the father of the child cried out, and said with tears, Lord, I believe; help thou mine unbelief.

MARK 9:23, 24

Looking unto Jesus the author and finisher of our faith; who for the joy that was set before him endured the cross, despising the shame, and is set down at the right hand of the throne of God.

HEBREWS 12:2

Now the birth of Jesus Christ was on this wise: When as his mother Mary was espoused to Joseph, before they came together, she was found with child of the Holy Ghost. Then Joseph her husband, being a just man, and not willing to make her a publick example, was minded to put her away privily. But while he thought on these things, behold, the angel of the Lord appeared unto him in a dream, saying, Joseph, thou son of David, fear not to take unto thee Mary thy wife: for that which is conceived in her is of the Holy Ghost. And she shall bring forth a son, and thou shalt call his name JESUS: for he shall save his people from their sins.

MATTHEW 1:18-21

And when Jesus was entered into Capernaum, there came unto him a centurion, beseeching him, And saying, Lord, my servant lieth at home sick of the palsy, grievously tormented. And Jesus saith unto him, I will come and heal him. The centurion answered and said, Lord, I am not worthy that thou shouldest come under my roof: but speak the word only, and my servant shall be healed. For I am a man under authority, having soldiers under me: and I say to this man, Go, and he goeth; and to another, Come, and he cometh; and to my servant, Do this, and he doeth it. When Jesus heard it, he marvelled, and said to them that followed, Verily I say unto you, I have not found so great faith, no, not in Israel. And Jesus said unto the centurion, Go thy way; and as thou hast believed, so be it done unto thee. And his servant was healed in the selfsame hour.

MATTHEW 8:5-10, 13

St. Peter's Church, pictured at left, stands in Jaffa, which is a part of Tel Aviv, Israel. Situated on a rocky ledge overlooking the Mediterranean, Jaffa, known as Joppa in Biblical times, was an important seaport and the home of Tabitha, a faithful woman who was raised from the dead by Simon Peter. (Photograph by Stockman/International Stock)

Ancient Egyptians referred to their country as Tawy, which translates to mean "the two lands." The name is an obvious reference to the dramatic difference between the fertile Nile Valley and the barren, sandy desert that makes up the remainder of the country. Much of this ancient land looks today as it did when Egypt was founded more than three thousand years before Christ's birth. Here, two Egyptian men look out over the desert landscape near Luxor, Egypt. (Photograph by E. Streichan/Superstock)

TRUST

Trust
in the LORD
with all
thine heart;
and lean
not unto
thine own
understanding.

PROVERBS 3:5

The LORD appeared to Abram, and said unto him, I am the Almighty God; walk before me, and be thou perfect. And I will make my covenant between me and thee, and will multiply thee exceedingly. And Abram fell on his face: and God talked with him, saying, As for me, behold, my covenant is with thee, and thou shalt be a father of many nations. Neither shall thy name any more be called Abram, but thy name shall be Abraham; for a father of many nations have I made thee. And I will make thee exceeding fruitful, and I will make nations of thee, and kings shall come out of thee. And I will establish my covenant between me and thee and thy seed after thee in their generations for an everlasting covenant, to be a God unto thee, and to thy seed after thee. And I will give unto thee, and to thy seed after thee, the land wherein thou art a stranger, all the land of Canaan, for an everlasting possession; and I will be their God. And God said unto Abraham, Thou shalt keep my covenant therefore, thou, and thy seed after thee in their generations.

GENESIS 17:1B-9

*Pictured above is Knossos on the Mediter-
ranean island of Crete. The Apostle Paul,
captive on a Roman ship, was shipwrecked
near the island and forced to swim to shore
in an incident described in Acts 27-28.
(Photograph by K. Scholz/Superstock)*

The modern city of Tel Aviv, pictured above, is located on the central Mediterranean coast of Israel and is the nation's largest district. Its name is from the ancient Babylonian region of Tel Abib, where the prophet Ezekiel spoke the word of God to the Jewish captives at the river Chebar. (Photograph by Buddy Mays/International Stock)

Now when Jesus was born in Bethlehem of Judaea in the days of Herod the king, behold, there came wise men from the east to Jerusalem, Saying, Where is he that is born King of the Jews? for we have seen his star in the east, and are come to worship him.

When Herod the king had heard these things, he was troubled, and all Jerusalem with him. And when he had gathered all the chief priests and scribes of the people together, he demanded of them where Christ should be born. And they said unto him, In Bethlehem of Judaea: for thus it is written by the prophet, And thou Bethlehem, in the land of Juda, art not the least among the princes of Juda: for out of thee shall come a Governor, that shall rule my people Israel. Then Herod, when he had privily called the wise men, enquired of them diligently what time the star appeared. And he sent them to Bethlehem, and said, Go and search diligently for the young child; and when ye have found him, bring me word again, that I may come and worship him also.

When they had heard the king, they departed; and, lo, the star, which they saw in the east, went before them, till it came and stood over where the young child was. When they saw the star, they rejoiced with exceeding great joy. And when they were come into the house, they saw the young child with Mary his mother, and fell down, and worshipped him: and when they had opened their treasures, they presented unto him gifts; gold, and frankincense, and myrrh. And being warned of God in a dream that they should not return to Herod, they departed into their own country another way.

MATTHEW 2:1-12

The LORD will perfect that which concerneth me: thy mercy, O LORD, endureth for ever: forsake not the works of thine own hands.

PSALM 138:8

And Jesus said unto them, I am the bread of life: he that cometh to me shall never hunger; and he that believeth on me shall never thirst.

JOHN 6:35

Consider the lilies of the field, how they grow; they toil not, neither do they spin: And yet I say unto you, That even Solomon in all his glory was not arrayed like one of these.

MATTHEW 6:28B, 29

Are not two sparrows sold for a farthing? and one of them shall not fall on the ground without your Father. But the very hairs of your head are all numbered. Fear ye not therefore, ye are of more value than many sparrows.

MATTHEW 10:29-31

Then I went down to the potter's house, and, behold, he wrought a work on the wheels. And the vessel that he made of clay was marred in the hand of the potter: so he made it again another vessel, as seemed good to the potter to make it. Then the word of the LORD came to me, saying, O house of Israel, cannot I do with you as this potter? saith the LORD. Behold, as the clay is in the potter's hand, so are ye in mine hand, O house of Israel.

JEREMIAH 18:3-6

Some trust in chariots, and some in horses: but we will remember the name of the LORD our God.

PSALM 20:7

Wherefore, if God so clothe the grass of the field, which to day is, and to morrow is cast into the oven, shall he not much more clothe you, O ye of little faith? Therefore take no thought, saying, What shall we eat? or, What shall we drink? or, Wherewithal shall we be clothed? . . . for your heavenly Father knoweth that ye have need of all these things. But seek ye first the kingdom of God, and his righteousness; and all these things shall be added unto you. Take therefore no thought for the morrow: for the morrow shall take thought for the things of itself. Sufficient unto the day is the evil thereof.

MATTHEW 6:30-34

For I am persuaded, that neither death, nor life, nor angels, nor principalities, nor powers, nor things present, nor things to come, Nor height, nor depth, nor any other creature, shall be able to separate us from the love of God, which is in Christ Jesus our Lord.

ROMANS 8:38, 39

Blessed is the man that trusteth in the LORD, and whose hope the LORD is. For he shall be as a tree planted by the waters, and that spreadeth out her roots by the river, and shall not see when heat cometh, but her leaf shall be green; and shall not be careful in the year of drought, neither shall cease from yielding fruit.

JEREMIAH 17:7, 8

The LORD is good, a strong hold in the day of trouble; and he knoweth them that trust in him.

NAHUM 1:7

But as it is written, Eye hath not seen, nor ear heard, neither have entered into the heart of man, the things which God hath prepared for them that love him.

I CORINTHIANS 2:9

In all thy ways acknowledge him, and he shall direct thy paths.

PROVERBS 3:6

The Dead Sea Scrolls were discovered in 1947 by a Bedouin shepherd searching for a stray member of his flock. In all, nearly five hundred scrolls and fragments were eventually uncovered in eleven caves on the Dead Sea's northwest coast. Pictured above is cave number six. Written by members of a Jewish community between 250 B.C. and A.D. 68, the Dead Sea Scrolls contain Biblical manuscripts and other documents relating to the Bible and the lives of the ancient authors. The Scrolls have proven to be one of the most valuable references for scholars studying the Bible and the history of the Biblical era. (Photograph by Buddy Mays/International Stock)

Therefore I say unto you, Take no thought for your life, what ye shall eat, or what ye shall drink; nor yet for your body, what ye shall put on. Is not the life more than meat, and the body than raiment? Behold the fowls of the air: for they sow not, neither do they reap, nor gather into barns; yet your heavenly Father feedeth them. Are ye not much better than they?

MATTHEW 6:25, 26

He that dwelleth in the secret place of the most High shall abide under the shadow of the Almighty. I will say of the LORD, He is my refuge and my fortress: my God; in him will I trust.

PSALM 91:1, 2

Lay not up for yourselves treasures upon earth, where moth and rust doth corrupt, and where thieves break through and steal: But lay up for yourselves treasures in heaven, where neither moth nor rust doth corrupt, and where thieves do not break through nor steal: For where your treasure is, there will your heart be also.

MATTHEW 6:19-21

Your Father knoweth what things ye have need of, before ye ask him.

MATTHEW 6:8B

Take no thought how or what ye shall speak: for it shall be given you in that same hour what ye shall speak. For it is not ye that speak, but the Spirit of your Father which speaketh in you.

MATTHEW 10:19B, 20

Delight thyself also in the LORD; and he shall give thee the desires of thine heart. Commit thy way unto the LORD; trust also in him; and he shall bring it to pass. And he shall bring forth thy righteousness as the light, and thy judgment as the noonday.

PSALM 37:4-6

The garden tomb above is located in Jerusalem, the city known in the Bible as "the City of David." Most scholars believe that the majority of the Book of Psalms was written by King David, and he is in fact named as the author in the introductions to over seventy of the individual psalms. The Book of Psalms contains some of the most beautiful and inspirational language in all of the Bible and carries an overall message of praise; individual psalms, however, cover topics as diverse as war, wisdom, and creation. (Photograph by A. Himmelreich/Superstock)

OLORD, thou hast searched me, and known me. Thou knowest my downsitting and mine uprising, thou understandest my thought afar off. Thou compassest my path and my lying down, and art acquainted with all my ways. For there is not a word in my tongue, but, lo, O LORD, thou knowest it altogether. Thou hast beset me behind and before, and laid thine hand upon me. Such knowledge is too wonderful for me; it is high, I cannot attain unto it.

Whither shall I go from thy spirit? or whither shall I flee from thy presence? If I ascend up into heaven, thou art there: if I make my bed in hell, behold, thou art there. If I take the wings of the morning, and dwell in the uttermost parts of the sea; Even there shall thy hand lead me, and thy right hand shall hold me. If I say, Surely the darkness shall cover me; even the night shall be light about me. Yea, the darkness hideth not from thee; but the night shineth as the day: the darkness and the light are both alike to thee. For thou hast possessed my reins: thou hast covered me in my mother's womb. I will praise thee; for I am fearfully and wonderfully made: marvellous are thy works; and that my soul knoweth right well. My substance was not hid from thee, when I was made in secret, and curiously wrought in the lowest parts of the earth. Thine eyes did see my substance, yet being unperfect; and in thy book all my members were written, which in continuance were fashioned, when as yet there was none of them.

How precious also are thy thoughts unto me, O God! how great is the sum of them! If I should count them, they are more in number than the sand: when I awake, I am still with thee. Search me, O God, and know my heart: try me, and know my thoughts: And see if there be any wicked way in me, and lead me in the way everlasting.

PSALM 139:1-18, 23, 24

At the height of Greek civilization, Athens was the cultural center of the ancient world. It was during this period of prosperity that the Parthenon was built to honor the Greek goddess Athena in the fifth century B.C. The building stood strong for centuries until its interior was destroyed by an explosion during a battle between the Greeks and the Venetians in 1687. The ruins of the Parthenon, pictured above, stand on the Acropolis high above modern Athens. (Photograph by P. Amranand/Superstock)

HUMBLENESS

The LORD
seeth not
as man seeth;
for man looketh
on the outward
appearance,
but the LORD
looketh on
the heart.

I Samuel 16:7b

Take heed that ye do not your alms before men, to be seen of them: otherwise ye have no reward of your Father which is in heaven. Therefore when thou doest thine alms, do not sound a trumpet before thee, as the hypocrites do in the synagogues and in the streets, that they may have glory of men. Verily I say unto you, They have their reward. But when thou doest alms, let not thy left hand know what thy right hand doeth: That thine alms may be in secret: and thy Father which seeth in secret himself shall reward thee openly.

MATTHEW 6:1-4

Likewise, ye younger, submit yourselves unto the elder. Yea, all of you be subject one to another; and be clothed with humility: for God resisteth the proud, and giveth grace to the humble. Humble yourselves therefore under the mighty hand of God, that he may exalt you in due time.

I PETER 5:5, 6

Let this mind be in you, which was also in Christ Jesus: Who, being in the form of God, thought it not robbery to be equal with God: But made himself of no reputation, and took upon him the form of a servant, and was made in the likeness of men: And being found in fashion as a man, he humbled himself, and became obedient unto death, even the death of the cross.

PHILIPPIANS 2:5-8

Yea, the stork in the heaven knoweth her appointed times; and the turtle and the crane and the swallow observe the time of their coming; but my people know not the judgment of the LORD.

JEREMIAH 8:7

Boast not thyself of to morrow; for thou knowest not what a day may bring forth. Let another man praise thee, and not thine own mouth; a stranger, and not thine own lips.

PROVERBS 27:1, 2

Vanity of vanities, saith the preacher; all is vanity.

ECCLESIASTES 12:8

And a certain scribe came, and said unto him, Master, I will follow thee whithersoever thou goest. And Jesus saith unto him, The foxes have holes, and the birds of the air have nests; but the Son of man hath not where to lay his head.

MATTHEW 8:19, 20

But so shall it not be among you: but whosoever will be great among you, shall be your minister: And whosoever of you will be the chiefest, shall be servant of all. For even the Son of man came not to be ministered unto, but to minister, and to give his life a ransom for many.

MARK 10:43-45

When thou art bidden of any man to a wedding, sit not down in the highest room; lest a more honourable man than thou be bidden of him; And he that bade thee and him come and say to thee, Give this man place; and thou begin with shame to take the lowest room. But when thou art bidden, go and sit down in the lowest room; that when he that bade thee cometh, he may say unto thee, Friend, go up higher: then shalt thou have worship in the presence of them that sit at meat with thee. For whosoever exalteth himself shall be abased; and he that humbleth himself shall be exalted.

LUKE 14:8-11

So after he had washed their feet, and had taken his garments, and was set down again, he said unto them, Know ye what I have done to you? Ye call me Master and Lord: and ye say well; for so I am. If I then, your Lord and Master, have washed your feet; ye also ought to wash one another's feet. For I have given you an example, that ye should do as I have done to you. Verily, verily, I say unto you, The servant is not greater than his lord; neither he that is sent greater than he that sent him. If ye know these things, happy are ye if ye do them.

JOHN 13:12-17

The city of Rome was the capital of the vast Roman Empire which, during the years before and after the birth of Jesus Christ, spread to the far corners of the ancient world. The majestic ruins of the Roman Forum, above, stand today as a testament to the power and the glory that was once Rome. According to tradition, the legendary city's founder, Romulus, was buried somewhere in the Forum. (Photograph by G. Barone/Superstock)

PRAYER

Seek ye
the LORD
while he may
be found,
call ye upon
him while
he is near.

ISAIAH 55:6

Our Father which art in heaven, Hallowed be thy name. Thy kingdom come. Thy will be done in earth, as it is in heaven. Give us this day our daily bread. And forgive us our debts, as we forgive our debtors. And lead us not into temptation, but deliver us from evil: For thine is the kingdom, and the power, and the glory, for ever. Amen.

MATTHEW 6:9B-13

Pictured above is Wadi Rum in Jordan, the modern nation that lies east of the Jordan River. In the Old Testament, the Hebrew people reached the eastern shore of the Jordan after their years of captivity and wandering; crossing the river symbolized their long-awaited arrival in the Promised Land. (Photograph by H. Kanus/Superstock)

These words spake Jesus, and lifted up his eyes to heaven, and said, Father, the hour is come; glorify thy Son, that thy Son also may glorify thee: As thou hast given him power over all flesh, that he should give eternal life to as many as thou hast given him. And this is life eternal, that they might know thee the only true God, and Jesus Christ, whom thou hast sent. I have glorified thee on the earth: I have finished the work which thou gavest me to do. And now, O Father, glorify thou me with thine own self with the glory which I had with thee before the world was.

I have manifested thy name unto the men which thou gavest me out of the world: thine they were, and thou gavest them me; and they have kept thy word. Now they have known that all things whatsoever thou hast given me are of thee. For I have given unto them the words which thou gavest me; and they have received them, and have known surely that I came out from thee, and they have believed that thou didst send me. I pray for them: I pray not for the world, but for them which thou hast given me; for they are thine. And all mine are thine, and thine are mine; and I am glorified in them. And now I am no more in the world, but these are in the world, and I come to thee.

Holy Father, keep through thine own name those whom thou hast given me, that they may be one, as we are. While I was with them in the world, I kept them in thy name: those that thou gavest me I have kept, and none of them is lost, but the son of perdition; that the scripture might be fulfilled. And now come I to thee; and these things I speak in the world, that they might have my joy fulfilled in themselves. I have given them thy word; and the world hath hated them, because they are not of the world, even as I am not of the world. I pray not that thou shouldest take them out of the world, but that thou shouldest keep them from the evil. They are not of the world, even as I am not of the world. Sanctify them through thy truth: thy word is truth. As thou hast sent me into the world, even so have I also sent them into the world. And for their sakes I sanctify myself, that they also might be sanctified through the truth.

Neither pray I for these alone, but for them also which shall believe on me through their word; That they all may be one; as thou, Father, art in me, and I in thee, that they also may be one in us: that the world may believe that thou hast sent me. And the glory which thou gavest me I have given them; that they may be one, even as we are one: I in them, and thou in me, that they may be made perfect in one; and that the world may know that thou hast sent me, and hast loved them, as thou hast loved me. Father, I will that they also, whom thou hast given me, be with me where I am; that they may behold my glory, which thou hast given me: for thou lovedst me before the foundation of the world. O righteous Father, the world hath not known thee: but I have known thee, and these have known that thou hast sent me. And I have declared unto them thy name, and will declare it: that the love wherewith thou hast loved me may be in them, and I in them.

JOHN 17

Hear, O LORD, when I cry with my voice: have mercy also upon me, and answer me. When thou saidst, Seek ye my face; my heart said unto thee, Thy face, LORD, will I seek. Hide not thy face far from me; put not thy servant away in anger: thou hast been my help; leave me not, neither forsake me, O God of my salvation.

PSALM 27:7-9

Therefore I say unto you, What things soever ye desire, when ye pray, believe that ye receive them, and ye shall have them.

MARK 11:24

Watch and pray, that ye enter not into temptation: the spirit indeed is willing, but the flesh is weak.

MATTHEW 26:41

Confess your faults one to another, and pray one for another, that ye may be healed. The effectual fervent prayer of a righteous man availeth much.

JAMES 5:16

And in that day ye shall ask me nothing. Verily, verily, I say unto you, Whatsoever ye shall ask the Father in my name, he will give it you. Hitherto have ye asked nothing in my name: ask, and ye shall receive, that your joy may be full.

JOHN 16:23, 24

And he spake a parable unto them to this end, that men ought always to pray, and not to faint.

LUKE 18:1

But thou, when thou prayest, enter into thy closet, and when thou hast shut thy door, pray to thy Father which is in secret; and thy Father which seeth in secret shall reward thee openly.

MATTHEW 6:6

Whatsoever ye shall ask of the Father in my name, he may give it you.

JOHN 15:16B

And all things, whatsoever ye shall ask in prayer, believing, ye shall receive.

MATTHEW 21:22

Again I say unto you, That if two of you shall agree on earth as touching any thing that they shall ask, it shall be done for them of my Father which is in heaven. For where two or three are gathered together in my name, there am I in the midst of them.

MATTHEW 18:19, 20

Ask, and it shall be given you; seek, and ye shall find; knock, and it shall be opened unto you: For every one that asketh receiveth; and he that seeketh findeth; and to him that knocketh it shall be opened.

MATTHEW 7:7, 8

Then shall ye call upon me, and ye shall go and pray unto me, and I will hearken unto you. And ye shall seek me, and find me, when ye shall search for me with all your heart.

JEREMIAH 29:12, 13

And he went a little further, and fell on his face, and prayed, saying, O my Father, if it be possible, let this cup pass from me: nevertheless not as I will, but as thou wilt.

MATTHEW 26:39

And said unto them, It is written, My house shall be called the house of prayer; but ye have made it a den of thieves.

MATTHEW 21:13

God be merciful unto us, and bless us; and cause his face to shine upon us.

PSALM 67:1A

Acropolis *is the Greek word for a raised and fortified plateau within a city. Athens boasts the most famous acropolis in Greece; but the area surrounding the acropolis above, once in the ancient city of Corinth, holds spectacular ruins as well. Modern Corinth, located a few miles from the ruins, is only a small town, not at all like the thriving trade city that Corinth was in Biblical times. (Photograph by B. G. Silberstein/Superstock)*

FORGIVENESS

Be ye
therefore
merciful, as
your Father
also is
merciful.

LUKE 6:36

In those days came John the Baptist, preaching in the wilderness of Judaea, And saying, Repent ye: for the kingdom of heaven is at hand. For this is he that was spoken of by the prophet Esaias, saying, The voice of one crying in the wilderness, Prepare ye the way of the Lord, make his paths straight. And the same John had his raiment of camel's hair, and a leathern girdle about his loins; and his meat was locusts and wild honey. Then went out to him Jerusalem, and all Judaea, and all the region round about Jordan, And were baptized of him in Jordan, confessing their sins.

MATTHEW 3:1-6

Above is a stretch of the Jordan River in Jordan that is believed by scholars to be the site where John the Baptist baptized Jesus. John, who warned the people to "prepare ye the way of the Lord," himself prepared the way for Jesus; when John the Baptist was arrested, Jesus began His own ministry, fulfilling all that John the Baptist had promised. (Photograph by G. Ricatto/Superstock)

Scholars believe that a large Christian settlement once existed in the ancient city of Gerasa, above, which was located southeast of the Sea of Galilee. The modern name for the city is Jarash, and it is the site of some of the most well-preserved Roman ruins in Jordan. (Photograph by D. Von Knobloch/Superstock)

And the scribes and Pharisees brought unto him a woman taken in adultery; and when they had set her in the midst, They say unto him, Master, this woman was taken in adultery, in the very act. Now Moses in the law commanded us, that such should be stoned: but what sayest thou? This they said, tempting him, that they might have to accuse him. But Jesus stooped down, and with his finger wrote on the ground, as though he heard them not. So when they continued asking him, he lifted up himself, and said unto them, He that is without sin among you, let him first cast a stone at her. And again he stooped down, and wrote on the ground. And they which heard it, being convicted by their own conscience, went out one by one, beginning at the eldest, even unto the last: and Jesus was left alone, and the woman standing in the midst. When Jesus had lifted up himself, and saw none but the woman, he said unto her, Woman, where are those thine accusers? hath no man condemned thee? She said, No man, Lord. And Jesus said unto her, Neither do I condemn thee: go, and sin no more.

JOHN 8:3-11

Be ye angry, and sin not:
let not the sun go down
upon your wrath.

EPHESIANS 4:26

Judge not, and ye shall not be judged:
condemn not, and ye shall not be condemned:
forgive, and ye shall be forgiven: Give, and it shall
be given unto you; good measure, pressed down,
and shaken together, and running over, shall men
give into your bosom. For with the same measure
that ye mete withal it shall be
measured to you again.

LUKE 6:37, 38

Therefore we are buried
with him by baptism into
death: that like as Christ
was raised up from the
dead by the glory of the
Father, even so we also
should walk in newness
of life.

ROMANS 6:4

If we confess our sins, he is faithful and just
to forgive us our sins, and to cleanse us
from all unrighteousness.

I JOHN 1:9

And when ye stand praying, forgive,
if ye have ought against any:
that your Father also which is in heaven may
forgive you your trespasses.

MARK 11:25

Come now, and let us reason
together, saith the LORD:
though your sins be as
scarlet, they shall be as
white as snow;
though they be red like
crimson, they shall
be as wool.

ISAIAH 1:18

Wherefore I say unto you, All manner of sin and blasphemy shall be forgiven unto men: but the blasphemy against the Holy Ghost shall not be forgiven unto men.

MATTHEW 12:31

Therefore if any man be in Christ, he is a new creature: old things are passed away; behold, all things are become new.

II CORINTHIANS 5:17

Then came Peter to him, and said, Lord, how oft shall my brother sin against me, and I forgive him? till seven times? Jesus saith unto him, I say not unto thee, Until seven times: but, Until seventy times seven.

MATTHEW 18:21, 22

I indeed baptize you with water unto repentance: but he that cometh after me is mightier than I, whose shoes I am not worthy to bear: he shall baptize you with the Holy Ghost, and with fire.

MATTHEW 3:11

Who forgiveth all thine iniquities; who healeth all thy diseases.

PSALM 103:3

Forbearing one another, and forgiving one another, if any man have a quarrel against any: even as Christ forgave you, so also do ye.

COLOSSIANS 3:13

In the cultures of the ancient world, books of proverbs were frequently compiled by authors hoping to gather together the wisdom of their age. The Biblical Book of Proverbs follows closely upon this form, with the addition of God as a unifying theme. Proverbs is believed by scholars to have been compiled and written by King Solomon, known throughout the Holy Land as the wisest man ever to live. Above, shepherds watch over their flocks near Hatra, Iraq. (Photograph by Superstock)

WISDOM

The fear
of the
LORD
is the
beginning
of knowledge.

PROVERBS 1:7A

*The Wailing Wall, pictured above, is believed to be the remains of the
western wall of Herod's Temple, destroyed by the Romans in A.D. 70. The
Wall has become an important shrine to modern Jews, who visit it to pray
and mourn the loss of their temple. According to legend, the dewdrops
that gather on the Wall are its tears of sympathy for the Jewish people.
(Photograph by Hal Kern/International Stock)*

In that night did God appear unto Solomon, and said unto him, Ask what I shall give thee. And Solomon said unto God, Thou hast shewed great mercy unto David my father, and hast made me to reign in his stead. Now, O LORD God, let thy promise unto David my father be established: for thou hast made me king over a people like the dust of the earth in multitude. Give me now wisdom and knowledge, that I may go out and come in before this people: for who can judge this thy people, that is so great? And God said to Solomon, Because this was in thine heart, and thou hast not asked riches, wealth, or honour, nor the life of thine enemies, neither yet hast asked long life; but hast asked wisdom and knowledge for thyself, that thou mayest judge my people, over whom I have made thee king: Wisdom and knowledge is granted unto thee; and I will give thee riches, and wealth, and honour, such as none of the kings have had that have been before thee, neither shall there any after thee have the like.

II CHRONICLES 1:7-12

Teach me thy way,
O LORD.

PSALM 27:11A

Thy word have I hid
in mine heart, that I
might not sin against
thee.

PSALM 119:11

The fool hath said in
his heart, There is
no God.

PSALM 14:1A

A wise son maketh
a glad father . . . .

PROVERBS 10:1B

Train up a child in the way he should go: and when he is
old, he will not depart from it.

PROVERBS 22:6

Thy word is a lamp
unto my feet, and a
light unto my path.

PSALM 119:105

And ye shall know the truth, and the truth shall make
you free.

JOHN 8:32

Ye are of God,
little children, and
have overcome
them: because
greater is he that is
in you, than he that
is in
the world.

I JOHN 4:4

My son, keep thy father's commandment, and forsake
not the law of thy mother: Bind them continually upon
thine heart, and tie them about thy neck. When thou
goest, it shall lead thee; when thou sleepest, it shall keep
thee; and when thou awakest, it shall talk with thee.
For the commandment is a lamp; and the law is light;
and reproofs of instruction are the way of life.

PROVERBS 6:20-23

A wise man will hear, and will increase learning; and a man of understanding shall attain unto wise counsels.

PROVERBS 1:5

And that from a child thou hast known the holy scriptures, which are able to make thee wise unto salvation through faith which is in Christ Jesus. All scripture is given by inspiration of God, and is profitable for doctrine, for reproof, for correction, for instruction in righteousness: That the man of God may be perfect, throughly furnished unto all good works.

II TIMOTHY 3:15-17

Where there is no vision, the people perish: but he that keepeth the law, happy is he.

PROVERBS 29:18

Give instruction to a wise man, and he will be yet wiser: teach a just man, and he will increase in learning. The fear of the LORD is the beginning of wisdom: and the knowledge of the holy is understanding. For by me thy days shall be multiplied, and the years of thy life shall be increased.

PROVERBS 9:9-11

Again, the kingdom of heaven is like unto a merchant man, seeking goodly pearls: Who, when he had found one pearl of great price, went and sold all that he had, and bought it.

MATTHEW 13:45, 46

No man can serve two masters: for either he will hate the one, and love the other; or else he will hold to the one, and despise the other. Ye cannot serve God and mammon.

MATTHEW 6:24

For the earth shall be filled with the knowledge of the glory of the LORD, as the waters cover the sea.

HABAKKUK 2:14

Be not deceived; God is not mocked: for whatsoever a man soweth, that shall he also reap. For he that soweth to his flesh shall of the flesh reap corruption; but he that soweth to the Spirit shall of the Spirit reap life everlasting.

GALATIANS 6:7, 8

Remember now thy Creator in the days of thy youth, while the evil days come not, nor the years draw nigh, when thou shalt say, I have no pleasure in them.

ECCLESIASTES 12:1

If any of you lack wisdom, let him ask of God, that giveth to all men liberally, and upbraideth not; and it shall be given him.

JAMES 1:5

Search the scriptures; for in them ye think ye have eternal life: and they are they which testify of me.

JOHN 5:39

Whoso loveth instruction loveth knowledge.

PROVERBS 12:1A

So that thou incline thine ear unto wisdom, and apply thine heart to understanding.

PROVERBS 2:2

And the rain descended, and the floods came, and the winds blew, and beat upon that house; and it fell not: for it was founded upon a rock. And every one that heareth these sayings of mine, and doeth them not, shall be likened unto a foolish man, which built his house upon the sand: And the rain descended, and the floods came, and the winds blew, and beat upon that house; and it fell: and great was the fall of it.

MATTHEW 7:25-27

The pyramids of Egypt, like those above in Cairo, are one of the great wonders of the ancient world. Pyramids were built over the tombs of nearly one hundred royal Egyptians, mostly during what is known as the Old Kingdom period of Egyptian history, which is dated between 2600 and 2200 B.C. By the time the Israelites began their captivity in Egypt, the Great Pyramids had already stood for many years. (Photograph by K. Gibson/Superstock)

SALVATION

He that believeth on the Son hath everlasting life.

JOHN 3:36A

Therefore being justified by faith, we have peace with God through our Lord Jesus Christ: By whom also we have access by faith into this grace wherein we stand, and rejoice in hope of the glory of God. And not only so, but we glory in tribulations also: knowing that tribulation worketh patience; And patience, experience; and experience, hope: And hope maketh not ashamed; because the love of God is shed abroad in our hearts by the Holy Ghost which is given unto us. For when we were yet without strength, in due time Christ died for the ungodly. For scarcely for a righteous man will one die: yet peradventure for a good man some would even dare to die. But God commendeth his love toward us, in that, while we were yet sinners, Christ died for us.

ROMANS 5:1-8

Above is one of Rome's crown jewels, the Colosseum. Built by the Emperors Vespasian and Titus between A.D. 72 and 80, the towering building's open center held battles to the death between competing gladiators, animals, or both. The Colosseum was carefully designed by its ancient engineers; it offered tiers of raised seating for the specatators and underground rooms and passageways for the waiting animals and competitors. (Photograph by S. Vidler/Superstock)

Herod has been called the great city builder, and Caesarea was one of his most successful endeavors. Begun in 22 B.C., the city took over a decade to build; and the results were no less than impressive. Artificial breakwaters were added to accomodate even the largest Roman ships, which helped to make the city a crucial shipping point for Asia and Europe. Where a tiny harbor had once stood, Herod created a thriving seaport. Pictured above are the ruins of ancient Caesarea today. (Photograph by Buddy Mays/International Stock)

And Saul, yet breathing out threatenings and slaughter against the disciples of the Lord, went unto the high priest, And desired of him letters to Damascus to the synagogues, that if he found any of this way, whether they were men or women, he might bring them bound unto Jerusalem. And as he journeyed, he came near Damascus: and suddenly there shined round about him a light from heaven: And he fell to the earth, and heard a voice saying unto him, Saul, Saul, why persecutest thou me? And he said, Who art thou, Lord? And the Lord said, I am Jesus whom thou persecutest: it is hard for thee to kick against the pricks. And he trembling and astonished said, Lord, what wilt thou have me to do? And the Lord said unto him, Arise, and go into the city, and it shall be told thee what thou must do. And the men which journeyed with him stood speechless, hearing a voice, but seeing no man. And Saul arose from the earth; and when his eyes were opened, he saw no man: but they led him by the hand, and brought him into Damascus. But Saul increased the more in strength, and confounded the Jews which dwelt at Damascus, proving that this is very Christ.

ACTS 9:1-8, 22

And when he was gone forth into the way, there came one running, and kneeled to him, and asked him, Good Master, what shall I do that I may inherit eternal life? And Jesus said unto him, Why callest thou me good? there is none good but one, that is, God. Thou knowest the commandments, Do not commit adultery, Do not kill, Do not steal, Do not bear false witness, Defraud not, Honour thy father and mother. And he answered and said unto him, Master, all these have I observed from my youth. Then Jesus beholding him loved him, and said unto him, One thing thou lackest: go thy way, sell whatsoever thou hast, and give to the poor, and thou shalt have treasure in heaven: and come, take up the cross, and follow me.

MARK 10:17-21

In the end of the sabbath, as it began to dawn toward the first day of the week, came Mary Magdalene and the other Mary to see the sepulchre. And, behold, there was a great earthquake: for the angel of the Lord descended from heaven, and came and rolled back the stone from the door, and sat upon it. His countenance was like lightning, and his raiment white as snow: And for fear of him the keepers did shake, and became as dead men. And the angel answered and said unto the women, Fear not ye: for I know that ye seek Jesus, which was crucified. He is not here: for he is risen, as he said. Come, see the place where the Lord lay. And go quickly, and tell his disciples that he is risen from the dead; and, behold, he goeth before you into Galilee; there shall ye see him: lo, I have told you.

MATTHEW 28:1-7

For he shall grow up before him as a tender plant, and as a root out of a dry ground: he hath no form nor comeliness; and when we shall see him, there is no beauty that we should desire him. He is despised and rejected of men; a man of sorrows, and acquainted with grief: and we hid as it were our faces from him; he was despised, and we esteemed him not. Surely he hath borne our griefs, and carried our sorrows: yet we did esteem him stricken, smitten of God, and afflicted. But he was wounded for our transgressions, he was bruised for our iniquities: the chastisement of our peace was upon him; and with his stripes we are healed. All we like sheep have gone astray; we have turned every one to his own way; and the LORD hath laid on him the iniquity of us all.

ISAIAH 53:2-6

But Mary stood without at the sepulchre weeping. Jesus saith unto her, Woman, why weepest thou? whom seekest thou? She, supposing him to be the gardener, saith unto him, Sir, if thou have borne him hence, tell me where thou hast laid him, and I will take him away. Jesus saith unto her, Mary. She turned herself, and saith unto him, Rabboni; which is to say, Master. Jesus saith unto her, Touch me not; for I am not yet ascended to my Father: but go to my brethren, and say unto them, I ascend unto my Father, and your Father; and to my God, and your God.

JOHN 20:11A, 15-17

That if thou shalt confess with thy mouth the Lord Jesus, and shalt believe in thine heart that God hath raised him from the dead, thou shalt be saved.

ROMANS 10:9

And said, Verily I say unto you, Except ye be converted, and become as little children, ye shall not enter into the kingdom of heaven.

MATTHEW 18:3

For all have sinned, and come short of the glory of God; Being justified freely by his grace through the redemption that is in Christ Jesus: Whom God hath set forth to be a propitiation through faith in his blood, to declare his righteousness for the remission of sins that are past, through the forbearance of God; To declare, I say, at this time his righteousness: that he might be just, and the justifier of him which believeth in Jesus.

ROMANS 3:23-26

I am the door: by me if any man enter in, he shall be saved, and shall go in and out, and find pasture. The thief cometh not, but for to steal, and to kill, and to destroy: I am come that they might have life, and that they might have it more abundantly. I am the good shepherd: the good shepherd giveth his life for the sheep.

JOHN 10:9-11

He came unto his own, and his own received him not. But as many as received him, to them gave he power to become the sons of God, even to them that believe on his name.

JOHN 1:11, 12

Even so we, when we were children, were in bondage under the elements of the world: But when the fulness of the time was come, God sent forth his Son, made of a woman, made under the law, To redeem them that were under the law, that we might receive the adoption of sons. And because ye are sons, God hath sent forth the Spirit of his Son into your hearts, crying, Abba, Father. Wherefore thou art no more a servant, but a son; and if a son, then an heir of God through Christ.

GALATIANS 4:3-7

For the wages of sin is death; but the gift of God is eternal life through Jesus Christ our Lord.

ROMANS 6:23

Jesus saith unto him, I am the way, the truth, and the life: no man cometh unto the Father, but by me. If ye had known me, ye should have known my Father also: and from henceforth ye know him, and have seen him.

JOHN 14:6, 7

And ye shall be hated of all men for my name's sake: but he that endureth to the end shall be saved.

MATTHEW 10:22

Be it known unto you all, and to all the people of Israel, that by the name of Jesus Christ of Nazareth, whom ye crucified, whom God raised from the dead, even by him doth this man stand here before you whole. This is the stone which was set at nought of you builders, which is become the head of the corner. Neither is there salvation in any other: for there is none other name under heaven given among men, whereby we must be saved.

ACTS 4:10-12

And brought them out, and said, Sirs, what must I do to be saved? And they said, Believe on the Lord Jesus Christ, and thou shalt be saved, and thy house.

ACTS 16:30, 31

Jesus answered and said unto her, Whosoever drinketh of this water shall thirst again: But whosoever drinketh of the water that I shall give him shall never thirst; but the water that I shall give him shall be in him a well of water springing up into everlasting life.

JOHN 4:13, 14

For he hath made him to be sin for us, who knew no sin; that we might be made the righteousness of God in him.

II CORINTHIANS 5:21

All things are delivered unto me of my Father: and no man knoweth the Son, but the Father; neither knoweth any man the Father, save the Son, and he to whomsoever the Son will reveal him.

MATTHEW 11:27

For God so loved the world, that he gave his only begotten Son, that whosoever believeth in him should not perish, but have everlasting life. For God sent not his Son into the world to condemn the world; but that the world through him might be saved. He that believeth on him is not condemned: but he that believeth not is condemned already, because he hath not believed in the name of the only begotten Son of God.

JOHN 3:16-18

For I delivered unto you first of all that which I also received, how that Christ died for our sins according to the scriptures; And that he was buried, and that he rose again the third day according to the scriptures.

I CORINTHIANS 15:3, 4

There is one body, and one Spirit, even as ye are called in one hope of your calling; One Lord, one faith, one baptism, One God and Father of all, who is above all, and through all, and in you all. But unto every one of us is given grace according to the measure of the gift of Christ.

EPHESIANS 4:4-7

Blessed be the Lord God of Israel; for he hath visited and redeemed his people.

LUKE 1:68

And when they were come to the place, which is called Calvary, there they crucified him, and the malefactors, one on the right hand, and the other on the left. Then said Jesus, Father, forgive them; for they know not what they do.

LUKE 23:33-34A

And he said unto Jesus, Lord, remember me when thou comest into thy kingdom. And Jesus said unto him, Verily I say unto thee, To day shalt thou be with me in paradise. And it was about the sixth hour, and there was a darkness over all the earth until the ninth hour. And the sun was darkened, and the veil of the temple was rent in the midst. And when Jesus had cried with a loud voice, he said, Father, into thy hands I commend my spirit: and having said thus, he gave up the ghost.

LUKE 23:42-46

Jesus cried with a loud voice, saying, Eloi, Eloi, lama sabachthani? which is, being interpreted, My God, my God, why hast thou forsaken me? And Jesus cried with a loud voice, and gave up the ghost. And the veil of the temple was rent in twain from the top to the bottom. And when the centurion, which stood over against him, saw that he so cried out, and gave up the ghost, he said, Truly this man was the Son of God.

MARK 15:34B, 37-39

Above, a sign marks the Via Dolorosa in Jerusalem. Via Dolorosa translates as the "way of sorrows"; and it has been traditionally believed to be the route that Jesus walked on His way to Calvary, where He was crucified. (Photograph by Buddy Mays/International Stock)

The island of Crete, above, surrounded by the Mediterranean Sea, is just over 150 miles in length and contains
some of the most beautiful scenery in all of the ancient
world. (Photograph by F. Manley/Superstock)

GLORY

For I know that my redeemer liveth, and that he shall stand at the latter day upon the earth.

JOB 19:25

The voice of him that crieth in the wilderness, Prepare ye the way of the LORD, make straight in the desert a highway for our God. Every valley shall be exalted, and every mountain and hill shall be made low: and the crooked shall be made straight, and the rough places plain: And the glory of the LORD shall be revealed, and all flesh shall see it together: for the mouth of the LORD hath spoken it. The voice said, Cry. And he said, What shall I cry? All flesh is grass, and all the goodliness thereof is as the flower of the field: The grass withereth, the flower fadeth: because the spirit of the LORD bloweth upon it: surely the people is grass. The grass withereth, the flower fadeth: but the word of our God shall stand for ever.

ISAIAH 40:3-8

Lift up your eyes to the heavens, and look upon the earth beneath: for the heavens shall vanish away like smoke, and the earth shall wax old like a garment, and they that dwell therein shall die in like manner: but my salvation shall be for ever, and my righteousness shall not be abolished.

ISAIAH 51:6

In the beginning was the Word, and the Word was with God, and the Word was God. The same was in the beginning with God. All things were made by him; and without him was not any thing made that was made. In him was life; and the life was the light of men. And the light shineth in darkness; and the darkness comprehended it not.

JOHN 1:1-5

Pictured above is the Caspian Sea in modern-day Iran. The area south of the Caspian Sea was once a part of the ancient nation of Media. Mentioned often throughout the Old Testament, the Medes had a tumultous history and were often involved in history-changing battles, including the defeat of Nineveh that led to the fall of the Assyrian Empire in 612 B.C. The Medes themselves were defeated by the Persians in 549 B.C.; yet Media's influence on their conquerors remained strong, and the dual name "the Medes and Persians" was used for ages. (Photograph by K. Scholz/Superstock)

And it came to pass in those days, that there went out a decree from Caesar Augustus, that all the world should be taxed. (And this taxing was first made when Cyrenius was governor of Syria.) And all went to be taxed, every one into his own city. And Joseph also went up from Galilee, out of the city of Nazareth, into Judaea, unto the city of David, which is called Bethlehem; (because he was of the house and lineage of David:) To be taxed with Mary his espoused wife, being great with child. And so it was, that, while they were there, the days were accomplished that she should be delivered. And she brought forth her firstborn son, and wrapped him in swaddling clothes, and laid him in a manger; because there was no room for them in the inn.

And there were in the same country shepherds abiding in the field, keeping watch over their flock by night. And, lo, the angel of the Lord came upon them, and the glory of the Lord shone round about them: and they were sore afraid. And the angel said unto them, Fear not: for, behold, I bring you good tidings of great joy, which shall be to all people. For unto you is born this day in the city of David a Saviour, which is Christ the Lord. And this shall be a sign unto you; Ye shall find the babe wrapped in swaddling clothes, lying in a manger. And suddenly there was with the angel a multitude of the heavenly host praising God, and saying, Glory to God in the highest, and on earth peace, good will toward men. And it came to pass, as the angels were gone away from them into heaven, the shepherds said one to another, Let us now go even unto Bethlehem, and see this thing which is come to pass, which the Lord hath made known unto us. And they came with haste, and found Mary, and Joseph, and the babe lying in a manger. And when they had seen it, they made known abroad the saying which was told them concerning this child. And all they that heard it wondered at those things which were told them by the shepherds. But Mary kept all these things, and pondered them in her heart. And the shepherds returned, glorifying and praising God for all the things that they had heard and seen, as it was told unto them.

LUKE 2:1-20

When Jesus came into the coasts of Caesarea Philippi, he asked his disciples, saying, Whom do men say that I the Son of man am? And they said, Some say that thou art John the Baptist: some, Elias; and others, Jeremias, or one of the prophets. He saith unto them, But whom say ye that I am? And Simon Peter answered and said, Thou art the Christ, the Son of the living God. And Jesus answered and said unto him, Blessed art thou, Simon Bar-jona: for flesh and blood hath not revealed it unto thee, but my Father which is in heaven. And I say also unto thee, That thou art Peter, and upon this rock I will build my church; and the gates of hell shall not prevail against it.

MATTHEW 16:13-18

For as many as are led by the Spirit of God, they are the sons of God. For ye have not received the spirit of bondage again to fear; but ye have received the Spirit of adoption, whereby we cry, Abba, Father. The Spirit itself beareth witness with our spirit, that we are the children of God: And if children, then heirs; heirs of God, and joint-heirs with Christ; if so be that we suffer with him, that we may be also glorified together.

ROMANS 8:14-17

Behold, I shew you a mystery; We shall not all sleep, but we shall all be changed, In a moment, in the twinkling of an eye, at the last trump: for the trumpet shall sound, and the dead shall be raised incorruptible, and we shall be changed. For this corruptible must put on incorruption, and this mortal must put on immortality. So when this corruptible shall have put on incorruption, and this mortal shall have put on immortality, then shall be brought to pass the saying that is written, Death is swallowed up in victory. O death, where is thy sting? O grave, where is thy victory?

I CORINTHIANS 15:51-55

For the Lord himself shall descend from heaven with a shout, with the voice of the archangel, and with the trump of God: and the dead in Christ shall rise first: Then we which are alive and remain shall be caught up together with them in the clouds, to meet the Lord in the air: and so shall we ever be with the Lord. Wherefore comfort one another with these words.

I THESSALONIANS 4:16-18

And as they were eating, Jesus took bread, and blessed it, and brake it, and gave it to the disciples, and said, Take, eat; this is my body. And he took the cup, and gave thanks, and gave it to them, saying, Drink ye all of it; For this is my blood of the new testament, which is shed for many for the remission of sins. But I say unto you, I will not drink henceforth of this fruit of the vine, until that day when I drink it new with you in my Father's kingdom.

MATTHEW 26:26-29

Wherefore God also hath highly exalted him, and given him a name which is above every name: That at the name of Jesus every knee should bow, of things in heaven, and things in earth, and things under the earth; And that every tongue should confess that Jesus Christ is Lord, to the glory of God the Father.

PHILIPPIANS 2:9-11

But this is that which was spoken by the prophet Joel; And it shall come to pass in the last days, saith God, I will pour out of my Spirit upon all flesh: and your sons and your daughters shall prophesy, and your young men shall see visions, and your old men shall dream dreams: And on my servants and on my handmaidens I will pour out in those days of my Spirit; and they shall prophesy: And I will shew wonders in heaven above, and signs in the earth beneath; blood, and fire, and vapour of smoke: The sun shall be turned into darkness, and the moon into blood, before that great and notable day of the Lord come: And it shall come to pass, that whosoever shall call on the name of the Lord shall be saved.

ACTS 2:16-21

When the Son of man shall come in his glory, and all the holy angels with him, then shall he sit upon the throne of his glory: And before him shall be gathered all nations: and he shall separate them one from another, as a shepherd divideth his sheep from the goats.

MATTHEW 25:31, 32

And then shall they see the Son of man coming in the clouds with great power and glory. And then shall he send his angels, and shall gather together his elect from the four winds, from the uttermost part of the earth to the uttermost part of heaven.

MARK 13:26, 27

For unto us a child is born, unto us a son is given: and the government shall be upon his shoulder: and his name shall be called Wonderful, Counsellor, The mighty God, The everlasting Father, The Prince of Peace.

ISAIAH 9:6

Beloved, now are we the sons of God, and it doth not yet appear what we shall be: but we know that, when he shall appear, we shall be like him; for we shall see him as he is. And every man that hath this hope in him purifieth himself, even as he is pure.

I JOHN 3:2, 3

But thou, Bethlehem Ephratah, though thou be little among the thousands of Judah, yet out of thee shall he come forth unto me that is to be ruler in Israel; whose goings forth have been from of old, from everlasting.

MICAH 5:2

For whosoever will save his life shall lose it; but whosoever shall lose his life for my sake and the gospel's, the same shall save it. For what shall it profit a man, if he shall gain the whole world, and lose his own soul? Or what shall a man give in exchange for his soul? Whosoever therefore shall be ashamed of me and of my words in this adulterous and sinful generation; of him also shall the Son of man be ashamed, when he cometh in the glory of his Father with the holy angels.

MARK 8:35-38

And there shall come forth a rod out of the stem of Jesse, and a Branch shall grow out of his roots: And the spirit of the LORD shall rest upon him, the spirit of wisdom and understanding, the spirit of counsel and might, the spirit of knowledge and of the fear of the LORD.

ISAIAH 11:1, 2

But Jesus said, Suffer little children, and forbid them not, to come unto me: for of such is the kingdom of heaven.

MATTHEW 19:14

For, behold, I create new heavens and a new earth: and the former shall not be remembered, nor come into mind.

ISAIAH 65:17

I am Alpha and Omega, the beginning and the end, the first and the last.

REVELATION 22:13

Not every one that saith unto me, Lord, Lord, shall enter into the kingdom of heaven; but he that doeth the will of my Father which is in heaven. Many will say to me in that day, Lord, Lord, have we not prophesied in thy name? and in thy name have cast out devils? and in thy name done many wonderful works?

MATTHEW 7:21, 22

Watch therefore: for ye know not what hour your Lord doth come. Therefore be ye also ready: for in such an hour as ye think not the Son of man cometh.

MATTHEW 24:42, 44

While he yet spake, behold, a bright cloud overshadowed them: and behold a voice out of the cloud, which said, This is my beloved Son, in whom I am well pleased; hear ye him.

MATTHEW 17:5

I am the LORD, and there is none else, there is no God beside me.

ISAIAH 45:5A

Heaven and earth shall pass away: but my words shall not pass away. But of that day and that hour knoweth no man, no, not the angels which are in heaven, neither the Son, but the Father. Take ye heed, watch and pray: for ye know not when the time is. For the Son of man is as a man taking a far journey, who left his house, and gave authority to his servants, and to every man his work, and commanded the porter to watch. Watch ye therefore: for ye know not when the master of the house cometh, at even, or at midnight, or at the cockcrowing, or in the morning: Lest coming suddenly he find you sleeping. And what I say unto you I say unto all, Watch.

MARK 13:31-37

Not far from where this shepherd tends to his flock lies the ancient city of Bethlehem. The city, which is mentioned in the Old Testament as early as the book of Genesis, was the home of King David of Israel and was thereafter known as the City of David. Bethlehem is most cherished by Christians as the birthplace of David's descendant, Jesus Christ. The site of Jesus' birth is marked today by the Church of the Nativity, which scholars believe occupies the very location of the manger that sheltered Mary the night her Child was born. (Photograph by G. Nalbandian/Superstock)